Illustrated

COIN DATING GUIDE

for the eastern world

by Albert Galloway

Colin R. Bruce II, Editor
David J. Ostrowski, Production Coordinator

1

It is the dim haze of mystery that
adds enchantment to pursuit. —
Rivarol.

**krause
publications**

Iola, Wisconsin 54990

COPYRIGHT MCMLXXXIV KRAUSE PUBLICATIONS, INC.
Library of Congress Catalog Card Number 84-082191
International Standard Book Number 0-87341-046-7

TABLE OF CONTENTS

Introduction

The identification of the style of numerals and dating system appearing on a coin can at times be quite instrumental in narrowing down the kingdom, state or province of origin. Familiarity with the various numerals appearing on the "Standard International Numeral Systems Chart", Chart A will prove to be rewarding.

The "Illustrated Coin Dating Guide" includes various illustrated exercises in coin dating for many typical coinages listed in the "Standard Catalog of World Coins" and the "Standard Guide to South Asian Coins and Paper Money".

The ability of quick and accurate coin dating will open an old avenue of communications to numismatists worldwide. Correspondence is invited in regards to the subject and all inquiries should be sent to:

Colin R. Bruce, Editor
Standard Catalog of World Coins
700 East State Street
Iola, Wisconsin 54990, U.S.A.

GENERAL
SECTION I

EXPLANATIONS OF DATING SYSTEMS
Era Systems

(AD) Christian Era — This dating system had its beginning with the birth of Christ and years are accumulated at 365 days each (except leap year). See "Solar Years", page 17.

(AH) Mohammedan Era — This dating system had its beginning in 622 (AD) and it is a Lunar (AH) system in accordance with the Islamic Calendar. Years are accumulated at 354 days each. See "Lunar Years", page 17.

As Lunar years are shorter than Solar years, you must first change a Lunar (AH) date to a Solar (SH) date before you can calculate the proper (AD) date. This is done as follows:

Lunar (AH) date -3.03% of Lunar (AH) date = Solar (SH) date

Now that the Solar (SH) date is known, you can perform the following mathematics to arrive at the proper (AD) date.

Solar (SH) date + 621 = (AD) date

(BE) Buddhist Era — This dating system had the most use in the Thailand/Siam and Vietnam/Annam areas. It had its beginning in 543 (BC) and to change a (BE) date to an (AD) do as follows:

(BE) date -543 = (AD) date

(CD) Cyclical Dating System — This is a recurring 60 year cycle system.

Chinese System — This dating system had its beginning in 2697 (BC) and was used primarily in China and Chinese influenced areas. The method to convert a (CD) date to an (AD) date is by use of the Chinese Calendar (Cyclical Date Chart) chart F.

First, you find a Chinese character at right on the coin which corresponds to one across the top of the chart. Then, the same is done only with the left characters looking down the left side of the chart. Where these two lines cross, there is a box which contains three dates. By using your SCWC, you can determine which date is the proper one for your coin.

The mathematics for changing a Chinese Cyclical Date (CD) to an (AD) is as follows:

(Cycle x 60 years) + cycle 'yr' -2697 = (AD) date

Some coins of Vietnam/Annam use the Chinese Cyclical Dating (CD) System and there is evidence that some coins of Bhutan have this dating.

Tibetan System — This system had its beginning in 966 (AD) and the best and easiest method of converting a Tibetan (CD) date to an (AD) date is by use of the "Tibetan Cyclical Date Chart" chart G.

First, find a pair of numbers on the coin which indicate the cycle. Then, there will be a one, or two digit number to indicate the year in that cycle when the coin was struck. For better visual explanation, see the examples on pages 46-48.

The mathematics for changing a Tibetan Cyclical Date (CD) to an (AD) date is as follows:

(Cycle x 60 years) + cycle 'yr' + 966 = (AD) date

(CS) Chula Sakarat Era — This dating system had its beginning in 638 (AD) and was used mostly in the Thailand/Siam and Burma areas. The mathematics to change a (CS) date to an (AD) date are as follows:

(CS) date + 638 = (AD) date

CHART A

STANDARD INTERNATIONAL NUMERAL SYSTEMS

Prepared especially for the Illustrated Coin Dating Guide
© 1984 By Krause Publications

	0	½	1	2	3	4	5	6	7	8	9	10	50	100	500	1000
WESTERN	0	½	1	2	3	4	5	6	7	8	9	10	50	100	500	1000
ROMAN			I	II	III	IV	V	VI	VII	VIII	IX	X	L	C	D	M
ARABIC-TURKISH	•	١/٢	١	٢	٣	٤	٥	٦	٧	٨	٩	١٠	٥٠	١٠٠	٥٠٠	١٠٠٠
MALAY—PERSIAN	•	١/٢	١	٢	٣	٤	٥	٦ or ٧	٧	٨	٩	١٠	٥٠	١٠٠	٥٠٠	١٠٠٠
EASTERN ARABIC	٥	½	١	٢	٣	٤	٥	٦	٧	٨	٩	١٠	٥١٠	١٠٠	٥١٠٠	١٠٠٠
HYDERABAD ARABIC	٥	١/٢	١	٢	٣	٤	٥	٦	٧	٨	٩	١٠	٥٠	١٠٠	٥٠٠	١٠٠٠
INDIAN (Sanskrit)	०	८/२	१	२	३	४	५	६	७	८	९	१०	४०	१००	४००	१०००
ASSAMESE	০	৬/২	১	২	৩	৪	৫	৬	৭	৮	৯	১০	৫০	১০০	৫০০	১০০০
BENGALI	০	৩/৩	১	২	৩	৪	৫	৬	৭	৮	৯	১০	৫০	১০০	৫০০	১০০০
GUJARATI	૦	૧/૨	૧	૨	૩	૪	૫	૬	૭	૮	૯	૧૦	૪૦	૧૦૦	૪૦૦	૧૦૦૦
KUTCH	૦	૧/૩	૧	૨	૩	૪	૫	૬	૭	૮	૯	૧૦	૪૦	૧૦૦	૪૦૦	૧૦૦૦
NAVANAGAR	૦	૧/૨	૧	૨	૩	૪	૫ or ૬	૬	૭	૮	૯	૧૦	૪૦	૧૦૦	૪૦૦	૧૦૦૦
NEPALESE	૦	૧/૩	૧૬	૨	૩	૪	૪૬ or	૬	૭	૮ or ૬	૯	૧૦	૪૦	૧૦૦	૪૦૦	૧૦૦૦
TIBETAN	༠	༡/༢	༡	༢	༣	༤	༥	༦	༧	༨	༩	༡༠	༤༠	༧༠༠	༤༠༠	༧༠༠༠
MONGOLIAN	০	০/১	০	১	২	৩	৪	৫	৬	৭	৮	৯০	৫০	০০০	৫০০	০০০০
BURMESE	၀	၁/၂	၁	၂	၃	၄	၅	၆	၇	၈	၉	၁၀	၅၀	၁၀၀	၅၀၀	၁၀၀၀
THAI-LAO	๐	๑/๒	๑	๒	๓	๔	๕	๖	๗	๘	๙	๑๐	๕๐	๑๐๐	๕๐๐	๑๐๐๐
JAVANESE	০		১	২	৩	৪	৫	৬	৭	৮	৯	১০	৫০	১০০	৫০০	১০০০
ORDINARY CHINESE JAPANESE-KOREAN	零	半	一	二	三	四	五	六	七	八	九	十	十五	百	百五	千
OFFICIAL CHINESE			壹	貳	叁	肆	伍	陸	柒	捌	玖	拾	拾伍	佰	佰伍	仟
COMMERCIAL CHINESE			〡	〢	〣	乂	〦	丄	丅	〨	夊	十	〦十	百	〦百	〡千
KOREAN		반	일	이	삼	사	오	육	칠	팔	구	십	오십	백	오백	천
GEORGIAN		ჴ	ბ	გ	დ	ე	ვ	ზ	ჱ	თ	◌	ი				
			⒑	⒛	⒊	⒋	⒌	⒍	⒎	⒏	⒐	⒑⒑	⒛⒛	⒊⒊	⒋⒋	⒌⒌
ETHIOPIAN	♦		፩	፪	፫	፬	፭	፮	፯	፰	፱	፲	፶	፻	፭፻	፲፻
			፳	፴	፵		፷	፸	፹	፺						
HEBREW			א	ב	ג	ד	ה	ו	ז	ח	ט	י	נ	ק	תק	
			כ	ל	מ	מ	נ	ס	ע	פ	צ	ר	ש or ש	ת	תר	שת
GREEK			Α	Β	Γ	Δ	Ε	Σ	Τ	Ζ	Η	Θ	Ι	Ν	Ρ	Ο	Α
			Κ	Λ	Μ	Ξ	Ο	Π		Σ	Τ	Υ	Χ	Ψ	Ω

(EE) Ethiopian Era — This dating system had its beginning nearly 8 years after the advent of (AD) dating. The mathematics to change an (EE) date to an (AD) date is as follows:

(EE) date + 8 = (AD) date

Note: As the (EE) dating system began 7 years and 8 months after the (AD) system, it is possible to have Ethiopian coins of two different dates for the same (AD) year.

(JE) Jewish Era — This dating system had its beginning at the time of creation (according to their religious beliefs), on October 7, 3761 (BC). The easiest way to convert the dates of Israeli coins to (AD) dates, is to use the "Hebrew Numerals and Dates" chart L.

The mathematics to change a (JE) date to an (AD) date is as follows:

(JE) date -3760 = (AD) date

(KE) Korean Era — This dating system had its beginning in 2333 (AD). The mathematics to change a (KE) date to an (AD) date is as follows:

(KE) date -2333 = (AD) date

(RS) Bangkok Era — This dating system had its beginning in 1781 (AD) and is used only in Thailand/Siam. The mathematics to change a (RS) date to an (AD) date is as follows:

(RS) date + 1781 = (AD) date

(SE) Saka Era — This dating system had its beginning on March 3, 78 (AD), and had wide usage in certain Indian Princely States and in Nepal. To change a (SE) date to an (AD) date, the mathematics are as follows:

(SE) date + 78 = (AD) date

(SH) Solar Hejira — This dating system is an Arabic Solar year system. It had its beginning in 622 (AD), the same as the (AH) system, but years are added according to Solar years (365 days) and not Lunar years (354 days).

The mathematics to change a (SH) year to an (AD) year are as follows:

(SH) date + 621 = (AD) date

(VS) Vikrama Samvat Era — This dating system had its beginning on October 18, 58 (BC) and had wide usage in certain Indian Princely States and in Nepal. To change a (VS) date to an (AD) date, the mathematics are as follows:

(VS) date -57 = (AD) date

The 'yr' dating of coins means that a coin was dated in some specific year during the time span of a kingdom, the reign of a ruler, or the duration of a republic. Therefore, if a coin was minted in some certain year during a span of years, to pin down the actual date of the coin you will need to know when that span began.

Another important thing, you will see that 1 is subtracted in the formulas for 'yr' dating and, for more information on this, see "Why Do We Subtract 1?", page 15.

To better understand this type dating and the formulas, it is necessary to know the following:

'yr' — This is the specific year during the reign of a ruler, or during the span of years of a republic in which the coin was actually minted.

(YR) — A major dating system where coins are dated according to some ruler's reign.

Accession date — This is the first year, or part of a year, of the reign of a new ruler. It is also the beginning year for the 'yr' numbers which appear on the coins minted during his reign.

Reign — The specific span of years the ruler remained in power. It is important for determining the Accession date and to determine which ruler was in power when the coin was minted.

(Yr Rep) — A major coin dating system where coins are dated according to the duration of some republic.

DATING SYSTEMS BY COUNTRY

Country			
Afghanistan	(AD) (AH) (SH) (YR)	(md) (nd)	
Algeria	(AD) (AH)	(md) (nd)	
Bahrain	(AH)	(dt) (md)	
Bangladesh		(dt)	
Bhutan	(AD) (CD)	(nd)	
Burma	(CS)	(dt)	
China/Empire	(AH) (CD) (YR)	(nd)	
China/Republic	(CD) (YrRep)	(nd)	
China/ Manchukuo	(YR)		
China/Sinkiang	(AH) (CD) (YR)	(nd)	
China/Soviets	(AD)	(dt) (md) (nd)	
China/Peoples Republic	(AD)		
China/Republic Taiwan	(YrRep)		
Comoros Rep.	(AD) (AH)		
Egypt	(AD) (AH) (YR)	(dt) (md)	
Ethiopia	(AD) (EE)		
India/Empires	(AH)	(nd)	
India/ Presidencies	(AD) (AH) (YR)	(dt) (md) (nd)	
Indian Princely States	(AD) (AH) (SE) (VS) (YR)	(dt) (md) (nd)	
India/British	(AD) (AH) (YR)	(dt) (md) (nd)	
India/Danish	(AD)		
India/Dutch	(AD)	(nd)	
India/French	(AD) (AH)	(nd)	
India/ Portuguese	(AD)	(nd)	
Indonesia/ Dutch	(AD) (AH)		
Iran	(AD) (AH) (SH)	(md)	
Iraq	(AH)	(dt) (md)	
Israel	(AD) (JE)	(md)	
Italy	(AD) (Yr D)	(md)	
Japan	(AD) (YR)	(md)	
Jordan	(AD) (AH)	(md)	
Kenya	(AD) (AH)	(md)	
Korea	(KK) (YR)		
Kuwait	(AD) (AH)	(dt) (md)	
Libya	(AH)	(dt) (md) (nd)	
Malaysia	(AD) (AH)	(nd)	
Maldive Islands	(AD) (AH)	(md)	
Mauritania	(AD) (AH)	(md)	
Mongolia	(AD) (YrRep)		
Morocco	(AD) (AH)	(md) (wa)	
Nepal	(SE) (VS)	(nd)	
Oman	(AD) (AH)	(md)	
Pakistan	(AD)		
Qatar	(AH)	(dt)	
Qatar & Dubai	(AH)	(dt) (md)	
Saudi Arabia	(AH) (YR)	(dt) (md)	
Somalia	(AD) (AH)	(dt) (md)	
Sudan	(AD) (AH)	(dt) (md)	
Tanzania/ German	(AD) (AH)	(md)	
Tanzania/ Zanzibar	(AH)		
Thailand/Siam	(AD) (AH) (BE) (CS) (RS)	(md) (nd)	
Tibet	(CD) (YR)	(nd)	
Tunisia	(AD) (AH)	(dt) (md)	
Turkey	(AD) (AH) (YR)	(dt) (md)	
Russia/ Caucasia	(AD) (AH)	(dt)	
Russia/Krim	(AH)		
Russia/ Turkestan	(AH)		
United Arab Emirates	(AH)	(dt) (md) (nd)	
Vietnam/ Annam	(CD) (YR)	(nd)	
Yemen Arab Rep.	(AD) (AH)	(dt) (md)	
Yemen/Quaiti	(AH)		
Yemen/ Democratic Republic	(AD) (AH)	(dt) (md)	

Beginning Year — This is the first year, or part of a year, in which a republic began. It is also 'yr' 1 of the republic.

(YR) Year of Reign — This is a system where coins are dated according to the reign of some emperor, king or ruler. The year, or part of a year, when the ruler assumed power is called the Accession year, and is 'yr' 1 of the reign. The 'yr' number found on the coin denotes the year during the reign when the coin was minted. You can establish the Accession year in various ways, depending on the coin, and the way it is listed in the SCWC. On some coins, the Accession date will be displayed on every coin minted during the reign. On others, you will need to refer to beginning of that particular section of the SCWC and find a list of rulers and their reigns. Occasionally, it is possible you will need to look up the information at the library. The worst situation is that you may never determine the proper Accession date because it is not known.

It is possible for coins to have two different 'yr' dates for the same (AD) year. Say a ruler died in mid-year, that year could have coins with a 'yr' number for the last year of his reign. In that same (AD) year, the new ruler could have 'yr' number 1 on coins for the first year of his reign. For example:

Japan 10 Sen, Y-29, Emperor Mutsuhito 'yr' 45 (1912)
Japan 10 Sen, Y-36, Emperor Yoshihito 'yr' 1 (1912)

Most countries using (YR) dating kept things quite orderly but others, such as some of the Arabic Influenced Countries and especially the Indian Princely States and Presidencies, had so many contradictions, restrikes, frozen dates and errors, that (YR) date conversions become quite difficult.

Due to the many different methods of (YR) date display, numeral systems used, and calendars used, the varied problems will be explained by use of examples.

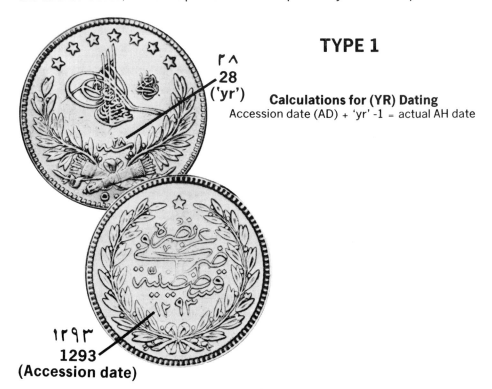

TYPE 1

٢٨
28
('yr')

Calculations for (YR) Dating
Accession date (AD) + 'yr' -1 = actual AH date

١٢٩٣
1293
(Accession date)

CHART C

CONVERSION TABLE
Various Dating Systems to (AD) Dates

(BE)	(CS)	(EE)	(JE)	(RS)	(SE)	(SH)	(VS)	(AD)	(BE)	(CS)	(EE)	(JE)	(RS)	(SE)	(SH)	(VS)	(AD)
2293	1112	1742			1672	1129	1807	1750	2355	1174	1804		31	1734	1191	1869	1812
2294	1113	1743			1673	1130	1808	1751	2356	1175	1805		32	1735	1192	1870	1813
2295	1114	1744			1674	1131	1809	1752	2357	1176	1806		33	1736	1193	1871	1814
2296	1115	1745			1675	1132	1810	1753	2358	1177	1807		34	1737	1194	1872	1815
2297	1116	1746			1676	1133	1811	1754	2359	1178	1808		35	1738	1195	1873	1816
2298	1117	1747			1677	1134	1812	1755	2360	1179	1809		36	1739	1196	1874	1817
2299	1118	1748			1678	1135	1813	1756	2361	1180	1810		37	1740	1197	1875	1818
2300	1119	1749			1679	1136	1814	1757	2362	1181	1811		38	1741	1198	1876	1819
2301	1120	1750			1680	1137	1815	1758	2363	1182	1812		39	1742	1199	1877	1820
2302	1121	1751			1681	1138	1816	1759	2364	1183	1813		40	1743	1200	1878	1821
2303	1122	1752			1682	1139	1817	1760	2365	1184	1814		41	1744	1201	1879	1822
2304	1123	1753			1683	1140	1818	1761	2366	1185	1815		42	1745	1202	1880	1823
2305	1124	1754			1684	1141	1819	1762	2367	1186	1816		43	1746	1203	1881	1824
2306	1125	1755			1685	1142	1820	1763	2368	1187	1817		44	1747	1204	1882	1825
2307	1126	1756			1686	1143	1821	1764	2369	1188	1818		45	1748	1205	1883	1826
2308	1127	1757			1687	1144	1822	1765	2370	1189	1819		46	1749	1206	1884	1827
2309	1128	1758			1688	1145	1823	1766	2371	1190	1820		47	1750	1207	1885	1828
2310	1129	1759			1689	1146	1824	1767	2372	1191	1821		48	1751	1208	1886	1829
2311	1130	1760			1690	1147	1825	1768	2373	1192	1822		49	1752	1209	1887	1830
2312	1131	1761			1691	1148	1826	1769	2374	1193	1823		50	1753	1210	1888	1831
2313	1132	1762			1692	1149	1827	1770	2375	1194	1824		51	1754	1211	1889	1832
2314	1133	1763			1693	1150	1828	1771	2376	1195	1825		52	1755	1212	1890	1833
2315	1134	1764			1694	1151	1829	1772	2377	1196	1826		53	1756	1213	1891	1834
2316	1135	1765			1695	1152	1830	1773	2378	1197	1827		54	1757	1214	1892	1835
2317	1136	1766			1696	1153	1831	1774	2379	1198	1828		55	1758	1215	1893	1836
2318	1137	1767			1697	1154	1832	1775	2380	1199	1829		56	1759	1216	1894	1837
2319	1138	1768			1698	1155	1833	1776	2381	1200	1830		57	1760	1217	1895	1838
2320	1139	1769			1699	1156	1834	1777	2382	1201	1831		58	1761	1218	1896	1839
2321	1140	1770			1700	1157	1835	1778	2383	1202	1832		59	1762	1219	1897	1840
2322	1141	1771			1701	1158	1836	1779	2384	1203	1833		60	1763	1220	1898	1841
2323	1142	1772			1702	1159	1837	1780	2385	1204	1834		61	1764	1221	1899	1842
2324	1143	1773			1703	1160	1838	1781	2386	1205	1835		62	1765	1222	1900	1843
2325	1144	1774		1	1704	1161	1839	1782	2387	1206	1836		63	1766	1223	1901	1844
2326	1145	1775		2	1705	1162	1840	1783	2388	1207	1837		64	1767	1224	1902	1845
2327	1146	1776		3	1706	1163	1841	1784	2389	1208	1838		65	1768	1225	1903	1846
2328	1147	1777		4	1707	1164	1842	1785	2390	1209	1839		66	1769	1226	1904	1847
2329	1148	1778		5	1708	1165	1843	1786	2391	1210	1840		67	1770	1227	1905	1848
2330	1149	1779		6	1709	1166	1844	1787	2392	1211	1841		68	1771	1228	1906	1849
2331	1150	1780		7	1710	1167	1845	1788	2393	1212	1842		69	1772	1229	1907	1850
2332	1151	1781		8	1711	1168	1846	1789	2394	1213	1843		70	1773	1230	1908	1851
2333	1152	1782		9	1712	1169	1847	1790	2395	1214	1844		71	1774	1231	1909	1852
2334	1153	1783		10	1713	1170	1848	1791	2396	1215	1845		72	1775	1232	1910	1853
2335	1154	1784		11	1714	1171	1849	1792	2397	1216	1846		73	1776	1233	1911	1854
2336	1155	1785		12	1715	1172	1850	1793	2398	1217	1847		74	1777	1234	1912	1855
2337	1156	1786		13	1716	1173	1851	1794	2399	1218	1848		75	1778	1235	1913	1856
2338	1157	1787		14	1717	1174	1852	1795	2400	1219	1849		76	1779	1236	1914	1857
2339	1158	1788		15	1718	1175	1853	1796	2401	1220	1850		77	1780	1237	1915	1858
2340	1159	1789		16	1719	1176	1854	1797	2402	1221	1851		78	1781	1238	1916	1859
2341	1160	1790		17	1720	1177	1855	1798	2403	1222	1852		79	1782	1239	1917	1860
2342	1161	1791		18	1721	1178	1856	1799	2404	1223	1853		80	1783	1240	1918	1861
2343	1162	1792		19	1722	1179	1857	1800	2405	1224	1854		81	1784	1241	1919	1862
2344	1163	1793		20	1723	1180	1858	1801	2406	1225	1855		82	1785	1242	1920	1863
2345	1164	1794		21	1724	1181	1859	1802	2407	1226	1856		83	1786	1243	1921	1864
2346	1165	1795		22	1725	1182	1860	1803	2408	1227	1857		84	1787	1244	1922	1865
2347	1166	1796		23	1726	1183	1861	1804	2409	1228	1858		85	1788	1245	1923	1866
2348	1167	1797		24	1727	1184	1862	1805	2410	1229	1859		86	1789	1246	1924	1867
2349	1168	1798		25	1728	1185	1863	1806	2411	1230	1860		87	1790	1247	1925	1868
2350	1169	1799		26	1729	1186	1864	1807	2412	1231	1861		88	1791	1248	1926	1869
2351	1170	1800		27	1730	1187	1865	1808	2413	1232	1862		89	1792	1249	1927	1870
2352	1171	1801		28	1731	1188	1866	1809	2414	1233	1863		90	1793	1250	1928	1871
2353	1172	1802		29	1732	1189	1867	1810	2415	1234	1864		91	1794	1251	1929	1872
2354	1173	1803		30	1733	1190	1868	1811	2416	1235	1865		92	1795	1252	1930	1873

This coin is an example where the Accession date, as well as the 'yr' is displayed on the coin. It is an Ottoman Turkish 500 Piastres, Y-40, coin minted during the reign of Abdul Hamid II (1293-1327 AH/1876-1909 AD). All coins minted during his reign displayed his Accession date.

With this coin, there are different methods of converting the numbers displayed to an (AD) date.

Method 1 — The easiest way to convert this (YR) date to an (AD) date is to recognize that it is in the (AH) dating system. Then, when the (AH) mint year is determined, look up the (AH) year in the "Hejira Date Chart D", and find the correct (AD) year. This can be done as follows:

$$\text{Accession date (AH)} + \text{'yr' (AH)} - 1 = \text{Mint date (AH)}$$
$$1293 + 28 - 1 = 1320 \text{ (AH)}$$

From the Hejira Date Chart 1320 (AH) = 1902 (AD)

Method 2 — Using this method, look up the Accession date (AD) of Abdulhamid II — 1876-1909 AD. Now, we cannot yet use the formula because we have the Accession date (1876 AD) in Solar years and the 'yr' number in Lunar years. So, as not to mix apples and oranges, we must correct the 'yr' number to the proper number of Solar years. As Lunar years are approximately 3% shorter than Solar years, subtract 3% from the number of Lunar years.

$$\text{Lunar years} \qquad -3\% \text{ of Lunar years} = \text{Solar years}$$
$$28 \qquad -.84 \text{ (make it 1)} = 27$$

We can now use our standard formula:

$$\text{Accession date (AD)} + \text{'yr' (AD)} - 1 = \text{Date (AD)}$$
$$1876 + 27 - 1 = 1902 \text{ (AD)}$$

Method 3 — This is the longhand method, and more complicated. First, the correct (AH) mint date must be found:

$$\text{Accession date (AH)} + \text{'yr'} - 1 = \text{Mint date (AH)}$$
$$1293 + 28 - 1 = 1320 \text{ (AH)}$$

Now we must change the Mint date (AH), which is a Lunar date, to a Mint date (SH) which is a Solar date.

$$\text{Mint date (AH)} \qquad -3.03\% \text{ of Mint date} = \text{Solar Mint date (SH)}$$
$$1320 \qquad -39 = 1281 \text{ (SH)}$$

As the correct Solar Mint date has been determined, it is simple to change this to the correct (AD) date.

$$\text{Date (SH)} \qquad + 621 = \text{Date (AD)}$$
$$1281 \qquad + 621 = 1902 \text{ (AD)}$$

Note: If you are a novice at (AH) dating, it is best to read and understand the following sections of this book:

CHANGING (AH) DATES TO (AD) DATES pages 17
LUNAR YEARS page 17
SOLAR YEARS page 17
WHY DO WE SUBTRACT 1? page 15

Type 2

This coin is an example where the Arabic numerals used for dating the coin are in accordance with Solar years, instead of Lunar years. The coin is a Nazarana Rupee, Y-13b, from the Indian Princely State of Jaipur. As you will see in your SGSAC & PM, it is listed under the rule of Madho Singh (1880-1922 AD). Another thing, when coins

CHART C

CONVERSION TABLE
Various Dating Systems to (AD) Dates

(BE)	(CS)	(EE)	(JE)	(RS)	(SE)	(SH)	(VS)	(AD)	(BE)	(CS)	(EE)	(JE)	(RS)	(SE)	(SH)	(VS)	(AD)
2417	1236	1866		93	1796	1253	1931	1874	2481	1300	1930		157	1860	1317	1995	1938
2418	1237	1867		94	1797	1254	1932	1875	2482	1301	1931		158	1861	1318	1996	1939
2419	1238	1868		95	1798	1255	1933	1876	2483	1302	1932		159	1862	1319	1997	1940
2420	1239	1869		96	1799	1256	1934	1877	2484	1303	1933		160	1863	1320	1998	1941
2421	1240	1870		97	1800	1257	1935	1878	2485	1304	1934		161	1864	1321	1999	1942
2422	1241	1871		98	1801	1258	1936	1879	2486	1305	1935		162	1865	1322	2000	1943
2423	1242	1872		99	1802	1259	1937	1880	2487	1306	1936		163	1866	1323	2001	1944
2424	1243	1873		100	1803	1260	1938	1881	2488	1307	1937		164	1867	1324	2002	1945
2425	1244	1874		101	1804	1261	1939	1882	2489	1308	1938		165	1868	1325	2003	1946
2426	1245	1875		102	1805	1262	1940	1883	2490	1309	1939		166	1869	1326	2004	1947
2427	1246	1876		103	1806	1263	1941	1884	2491	1310	1940	5708	167	1870	1327	2005	1948
2428	1247	1877		104	1807	1264	1942	1885	2492	1311	1941	5709	168	1871	1328	2006	1949
2429	1248	1878		105	1808	1265	1943	1886	2493	1312	1942	5710	169	1872	1329	2007	1950
2430	1249	1879		106	1809	1266	1944	1887	2494	1313	1943	5711	170	1873	1330	2008	1951
2431	1250	1880		107	1810	1267	1945	1888	2495	1314	1944	5712	171	1874	1331	2009	1952
2432	1251	1881		108	1811	1268	1946	1889	2496	1315	1945	5713	172	1875	1332	2010	1953
2433	1252	1882		109	1812	1269	1947	1890	2497	1316	1946	5714	173	1876	1333	2011	1954
2434	1253	1883		110	1813	1270	1948	1891	2498	1317	1947	5715	174	1877	1334	2012	1955
2435	1254	1884		111	1814	1271	1949	1892	2499	1318	1948	5716	175	1878	1335	2013	1956
2436	1255	1885		112	1815	1272	1950	1893	2500	1319	1949	5717	176	1879	1336	2014	1957
2437	1256	1886		113	1816	1273	1951	1894	2501	1320	1950	5718	177	1880	1337	2015	1958
2438	1257	1887		114	1817	1274	1952	1895	2502	1321	1951	5719	178	1881	1338	2016	1959
2439	1258	1888		115	1818	1275	1953	1896	2503	1322	1952	5720	179	1882	1339	2017	1960
2440	1259	1889		116	1819	1276	1954	1897	2504	1323	1953	5721	180	1883	1340	2018	1961
2441	1260	1890		117	1820	1277	1955	1898	2505	1324	1954	5722	181	1884	1341	2019	1962
2442	1261	1891		118	1821	1278	1956	1899	2506	1325	1955	5723	182	1885	1342	2020	1963
2443	1262	1892		119	1822	1279	1957	1900	2507	1326	1956	5724	183	1886	1343	2021	1964
2444	1263	1893		120	1823	1280	1958	1901	2508	1327	1957	5725	184	1887	1344	2022	1965
2445	1264	1894		121	1824	1281	1959	1902	2509	1328	1958	5726	185	1888	1345	2023	1966
2446	1265	1895		122	1825	1282	1960	1903	2510	1329	1959	5727	186	1889	1346	2024	1967
2447	1266	1896		123	1826	1283	1961	1904	2511	1330	1960	5728	187	1890	1347	2025	1968
2448	1267	1897		124	1827	1284	1962	1905	2512	1331	1961	5729	188	1891	1348	2026	1969
2449	1268	1898		125	1828	1285	1963	1906	2513	1332	1962	5730	189	1892	1349	2027	1970
2450	1269	1899		126	1829	1286	1964	1907	2514	1333	1963	5731	190	1893	1350	2028	1971
2451	1270	1900		127	1830	1287	1965	1908	2515	1334	1964	5732	191	1894	1351	2029	1972
2452	1271	1901		128	1831	1288	1966	1909	2516	1335	1965	5733	192	1895	1352	2030	1973
2453	1272	1902		129	1832	1289	1967	1910	2517	1336	1966	5734	193	1896	1353	2031	1974
2454	1273	1903		130	1833	1290	1968	1911	2518	1337	1967	5735	194	1897	1354	2032	1975
2455	1274	1904		131	1834	1291	1969	1912	2519	1338	1968	5736	195	1898	1355	2033	1976
2456	1275	1905		132	1835	1292	1970	1913	2520	1339	1969	5737	196	1899	1356	2034	1977
2457	1276	1906		133	1836	1293	1971	1914	2521	1340	1970	5738	197	1900	1357	2035	1978
2458	1277	1907		134	1837	1294	1972	1915	2522	1341	1971	5739	198	1901	1358	2036	1979
2459	1278	1908		135	1838	1295	1973	1916	2523	1342	1972	5740	199	1902	1359	2037	1980
2460	1279	1909		136	1839	1296	1974	1917	2524	1343	1973	5741	200	1903	1360	2038	1981
2461	1280	1910		137	1840	1297	1975	1918	2525	1344	1974	5742	201	1904	1361	2039	1982
2462	1281	1911		138	1841	1298	1976	1919	2526	1345	1975	5743	202	1905	1362	2040	1983
2463	1282	1912		139	1842	1299	1977	1920	2527	1346	1976	5744	203	1906	1363	2041	1984
2464	1283	1913		140	1843	1300	1978	1921	2528	1347	1977	5745	204	1907	1364	2042	1985
2465	1284	1914		141	1844	1301	1979	1922	2529	1348	1978	5746	205	1908	1365	2043	1986
2466	1285	1915		142	1845	1302	1980	1923	2530	1349	1979	5747	206	1909	1366	2044	1987
2467	1286	1916		143	1846	1303	1981	1924	2531	1350	1980	5748	207	1910	1367	2045	1988
2468	1287	1917		144	1847	1304	1982	1925	2532	1351	1981	5749	208	1911	1368	2046	1989
2469	1288	1918		145	1848	1305	1983	1926	2533	1352	1982	5750	209	1912	1369	2047	1990
2470	1289	1919		146	1849	1306	1984	1927	2534	1353	1983	5751	210	1913	1370	2048	1991
2471	1290	1920		147	1850	1307	1985	1928	2535	1354	1984	5752	211	1914	1371	2049	1992
2472	1291	1921		148	1851	1308	1986	1929	2536	1355	1985	5753	212	1915	1372	2050	1993
2473	1292	1922		149	1852	1309	1987	1930	2537	1356	1986	5754	213	1916	1373	2051	1994
2474	1293	1923		150	1853	1310	1988	1931	2538	1357	1987	5755	214	1917	1374	2052	1995
2475	1294	1924		151	1854	1311	1989	1932	2539	1358	1988	5756	215	1918	1375	2053	1996
2476	1295	1925		152	1855	1312	1990	1933	2540	1359	1989	5757	216	1919	1376	2054	1997
2477	1296	1926		153	1856	1313	1991	1934	2541	1360	1990	5758	217	1920	1377	2055	1998
2478	1297	1927		154	1857	1314	1992	1935	2542	1361	1991	5759	218	1921	1378	2056	1999
2479	1298	1928		155	1858	1315	1993	1936	2543	1362	1992	5760	219	1922	1379	2057	2000
2480	1299	1929		156	1859	1316	1994	1937									

are listed as, "In the Name of Queen Victoria", the dating is generally in accordance with Solar years and the date on the coin will often be a direct translation (dt) to the correct Mint date (AD).

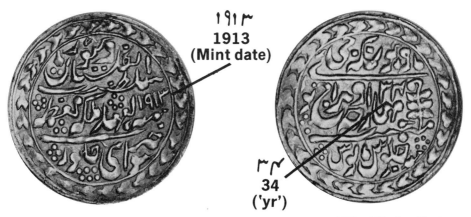

We can check this Mint date (AD) with the Accession date (AD) of Madho Singh, as follows:

Accession date (AD)   + 'yr' -1 = Mint date (AD)
1880   + 34 -1 = 1913 (AD)

Type 3

This coin displays only the 'yr' number on the coin, which is the most common method in most countries using the (YR)/'yr' method of coin dating. This coin is another from the Indian Princely State of Jaipur and is a ¼ Rupee, Y-11. As you will see in your SGSAC & PM, it also is listed under the rule of Madho Singh (1880-1922 AD). The 'yr' number on this coin is in Solar years. To find the Mint date (AD), do as follows:

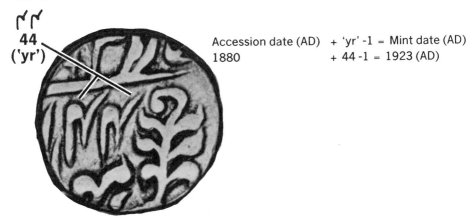

Accession date (AD)   + 'yr' -1 = Mint date (AD)
1880   + 44 -1 = 1923 (AD)

Other countries of the world, using (YR)/'yr' dating, have their systems well organized and will not be treated individually in these explanations. For more information, see the respective sections in this book. For a list of dating systems, see "Dating Systems by Country", chart B.

CHART D
HEBREW NUMERALS AND DATES

Hebrew Name	Cipher	Alternate Styles	Hebrew No.	A.D. Gregorian Date	Hebrew Year in ciphers	in letters
Alef	1		א	1948	5708	תש״ח
Bet	2		ב	1949	5709	תש״ט
Gimel	3		ג	1950	5710	תש״י
Dalet	4		ד	1951	5711	תשי״א
Hay	5	ו	ה	1952	5712	תשי״ב
Vov	6		ו	1953	5713	תשי״ג
Zayin	7		ז	1954	5714	תשי״ד
Het	8	ח	ח	1955	5715	תשט״ו
Tet	9	✓	ט	1956	5716	תשי״ו
Yod	10		י	1957	5717	תשי״ד
Kaf	20	ך	כ	1958	5718	תשי״ח or תשי״ח
Lamed	30		ל	1959	5719	תשי״ט or תשי״ט
Mem	40	ם	מ	1960	5720	תשר or תש״ך
Nun	50		נ	1961	5721	תשכ״א
Sameh	60		ס	1962	5722	תשכ״ב
	70		ע	1963	5723	תשכ״ג
	80		פ	1964	5724	תשכ״ד
	90		צ	1965	5725	תשכ״ה
	100		ק	1966	5726	תשכ״ו
	200		ר	1967	5727	תשכ״ז
	300	ש	ש	1968	5728	תשכ״ח
	400		ת	1969	5729	תשכ״ט
	500		תק	1970	5730	תש״ל
	600		תר	1971	5731	תשל״א
	700		שת	1972	5732	תשל״ב
				1973	5733	תשל״ג
				1974	5734	תשל״ד
				1975	5735	תשל״ה
				1976	5736	תשל״ו
				1977	5737	תשל״ז
				1978	5738	תשל״ח
				1979	5739	תשל״ט
				1980	5740	תש״ם
				1981	5741	התש מ״א
				1982	5742	התשמ״ב
				1983	5743	התש מ״ג
				1984	5744	התש מ״ד

' Separation mark
'' Separation mark

Note No. 1: — Sometimes the separation mark is left off coin dates.
Note No. 2: — On the 5720 (1960 AD) Agora coin, the bottom line (serif) is missing and appears as ך instead of כ.
Note: — Always read Hebrew dates from right to left.

Mathematics — (JE) date -3760 = (AD) date

EXPLANATIONS OF DATING SYSTEMS

(KK) Kingdom of Koryo/Yi Dynasty — This is a minor dating system used exclusively in Korea. It has been sufficiently explained in the section of this book, "Dates on Coins of Korea", pages 111-113.

(YrRep) Year of Republic — This dating system is similar to the (YR) system except it is based on the establishment and duration of some republic. To change a (YrRep) date to an (AD) date, it is necessary to determine the beginning year of that republic. For examples, refer to the proper section of this book.

Calculations for (YrRep) Dating
Beginning year of republic + 'yr' -1 = (AD) date
Note: See section, "Why Do We Subtract 1?", page 15.

*Various Date Types
(dt) Direct Translation — Many coins of the world, with dates in non-western numerals, often have date numbers which directly translate to the correct (AD) date. This is especially true amongst the Arabic Influenced Countries.

(md) Multiple Dates — Many coins, especially those of the Arabic Influenced Countries, have more than one dating system displayed on the same coin. Several of these have as many as three dating systems displayed.

(wa) Western To Arabic — With this system, the (AH) dates on coins are shown in western numerals. It is used almost exclusively to date Moroccan coins. The dates on the coins, even though displayed in western numerals, must be treated the same as any other (AH) date when changing it to an (AD) date.

(nd) No Date — Many coins of the world have no dates.

Minor Dating Systems
This is a list of Minor Dating Systems which will not be treated here-in:

(AM) Maludi Era	India Kingdom of Mysore
(AS) Aki Saka Era	Java
(FE) Fasli Era	India/Maratha Confederacy
(ME) Malabar Era	India, Princely State of Travancore
(MS) Monarchic Solar Era	Iran
(CB) Cooch Behar Era	India, Kingdom of Cooch Behar
(TE) Tripura Era	India, Princely State of Tripura

Why Do We Subtract 1?
The mathematical formulas for converting (YR) Year of Reign, (YrRep) Year of Republic, and (KK) Year of Kingdom dates to (AD) dates all show that 1 must be subtracted. Why is this? It is because the first year, or part of a year, is counted as 'yr' 1. An example would be:

Say a coin had a 'yr' number 3 on it (the third year of that Republic) and the beginning year of the Republic was 1911 (AD). Then:

'yr' 1 = 1911 (AD)
'yr' 2 = 1912 (AD)
'yr' 3 = 1913 (AD)

At first glance, it would seem that 'yr' 3 would be 1914 (AD), but that isn't the case. One year must be subtracted to make the (AD) date correct.

Why Isn't 1 Subtracted from the 'Era' Formulas?
Either the subtraction of 1 isn't required, or it has already been subtracted to make the formulas more simple to use.

CHART E — HEJIRA DATE CHART

HEJIRA (Hijra, Hegira), the name of the Mohammedan era (AH — Anno Hegirae) dates back to the Christian year 622 when Mohammed ''fled'' from Mecca, escaping to Medina to avoid persecution from the Koreish tribesmen. Based on a lunar year the Mohammedan year is 11 days shorter.

* — Leap Year (Christian Calendar)

AH	AD	AH	AD	AH	AD	AH	AD
957	1550, January 20	1040	1630, July 10	1122	1710, March 2	1205	1790, September 10
958	1551, January 9	1041	1631, July 30	1123	1711, February 19	1206	1791, August 30
959	1551, December 29	1042	1632, July 19*	1124	1712, February 9*	1207	1792, August 19*
960	1552, December 18*	1043	1633, July 8	1125	1713, January 28	1208	1793, August 9
961	1553, December 7	1044	1634, June 27	1126	1714, January 17	1209	1794, July 29
962	1554, November 26	1045	1635, June 17	1127	1715, January 7	1210	1795, July 18
963	1555, November 16	1046	1636, June 5*	1128	1715, December 27	1211	1796, July 7*
964	1556, November 4*	1047	1637, May 26	1129	1716, December 16*	1212	1797, June 26
965	1557, October 24	1048	1638, May 15	1130	1717, December 5	1213	1798, June 15
966	1558, October 14	1049	1639, May 4	1131	1718, November 24	1214	1799, June 5
967	1559, October 3	1050	1640, April 23*	1132	1719, November 14	1215	1800, May 25
968	1560, September 22*	1051	1641, April 12	1133	1720, November 2*	1216	1801, May 14
969	1561, September 11	1052	1642, April 1	1134	1721, October 22	1217	1802, May 4
970	1562, August 31	1053	1643, March 22	1135	1722, October 12	1218	1803, April 23
971	1563, August 21	1054	1644, March 10*	1136	1723, October 1	1219	1804, April 12*
972	1564, August 9*	1055	1645, February 27	1137	1724, September 29*	1220	1805, April 1
973	1565, July 29	1056	1646, February 17	1138	1725, September 9	1221	1806, March 21
974	1566, July 19	1057	1647, February 6	1139	1726, August 29	1222	1807, March 11
975	1567, July 8	1058	1648, January 27*	1140	1727, August 19	1223	1808, February 28*
976	1568, June 26*	1059	1649, January 15	1141	1728, August 7*	1224	1809, February 16
977	1569, June 16	1060	1650, January 4	1142	1729, July 27	1225	1810, February 6
978	1570, June 5	1061	1650, December 25	1143	1730, July 17	1226	1811, January 26
979	1571, May 26	1062	1651, December 14	1144	1731, July 6	1227	1812, January 16*
980	1572, May 14*	1063	1652, December 2*	1145	1732, June 24*	1228	1813, January 4
981	1573, May 3	1064	1653, November 22	1146	1733, June 14	1229	1813, December 24
982	1574, April 28	1065	1654, November 11	1147	1734, June 3	1230	1814, December 14
983	1575, April 12	1066	1655, October 31	1148	1735, May 24	1231	1815, December 3
984	1576, March 31*	1067	1656, October 20*	1149	1736, May 12*	1232	1816, November 21*
985	1577, March 21	1068	1657, October 9	1150	1737, May 1	1233	1817, November 11
986	1578, March 10	1069	1658, September 29	1151	1738, April 21	1234	1818, October 31
987	1579, February 27	1070	1659, September 18	1152	1739, April 10	1235	1819, October 20
988	1580, February 17*	1071	1660, September 6*	1153	1740, March 29*	1236	1820, October 9*
989	1581, February 5	1072	1661, August 27	1154	1741, March 19	1237	1821, September 28
990	1582, January 26	1073	1662, August 16	1155	1742, March 8	1238	1822, September 18
991	1583, January 25	1074	1663, August 5	1156	1743, February 25	1239	1823, September 7
992	1584, January 14*	1075	1664, July 25*	1157	1744, February 15*	1240	1824, August 26*
993	1585, January 3	1076	1665, July 14	1158	1745, February 3	1241	1825, August 16
994	1585, December 23	1077	1666, July 4	1159	1746, January 24	1242	1826, August 5
995	1586, December 12	1078	1667, June 23	1160	1747, January 13	1243	1827, July 25
996	1587, December 2	1079	1668, June 11*	1161	1748, January 2*	1244	1828, July 14*
997	1588, November 20*	1080	1669, June 1	1162	1748, December 22*	1245	1829, July 3
998	1589, November 10	1081	1670, May 21	1163	1749, December 11	1246	1830, June 22
999	1590, October 30	1082	1671, May 10	1164	1750, November 30	1247	1831, June 12
1000	1591, October 19	1083	1672, April 29*	1165	1751, November 20	1248	1832, May 31*
1001	1592, October 8*	1084	1673, April 18	1166	1752, November 8*	1249	1833, May 21
1002	1593, September 27	1085	1674, April 7	1167	1753, October 29	1250	1834, May 10
1003	1594, September 16	1086	1675, March 28	1168	1754, October 18	1251	1835, April 29
1004	1595, September 6	1087	1676, March 16*	1169	1755, October 7	1252	1836, April 18*
1005	1596, August 26*	1088	1677, March 6	1170	1756, September 26*	1253	1837, April 7
1006	1597, August 14	1089	1678, February 23	1171	1757, September 15	1254	1838, March 27
1007	1598, August 4	1090	1679, February 12	1172	1758, September 4	1255	1839, March 17
1008	1599, July 24	1091	1680, February 2*	1173	1759, August 25	1256	1840, March 5*
1009	1600, July 13*	1092	1681, January 21	1174	1760, August 13*	1257	1841, February 23
1010	1601, July 2	1093	1682, January 10	1175	1761, August 2	1258	1842, February 12
1011	1602, June 21	1094	1682, December 31	1176	1762, July 23	1259	1843, February 1
1012	1603, June 11	1095	1683, December 20	1177	1763, July 12	1260	1844, January 22*
1013	1604, May 30*	1096	1684, December 8*	1178	1764, July 1*	1261	1845, January 10
1014	1605, May 19	1097	1685, November 28	1179	1765, June 20	1262	1845, December 30
1015	1606, May 9	1098	1686, November 17	1180	1766, June 9	1263	1846, December 20
1016	1607, April 28	1099	1687, November 7	1181	1767, May 30	1264	1847, December 9
1017	1608, April 16*	1100	1688, October 26*	1182	1768, May 18*	1265	1848, November 27*
1018	1609, April 6	1101	1689, October 15	1183	1769, May 7	1266	1849, November 17
1019	1610, March 26	1102	1690, October 5	1184	1770, April 27	1267	1850, November 6
1020	1611, March 16	1103	1691, September 24	1185	1771, April 16	1268	1851, October 27
1021	1612, March 4*	1104	1692, September 12*	1186	1772, April 4*	1269	1852, October 15*
1022	1613, February 21	1105	1693, September 2	1187	1773, March 25	1270	1853, October 4
1023	1614, February 11	1106	1694, August 22	1188	1774, March 14	1271	1854, September 24
1024	1615, January 31	1107	1695, August 12	1189	1775, March 4	1272	1855, September 13
1025	1616, January 20*	1108	1696, July 31*	1190	1776, February 21*	1273	1856, September 1*
1026	1617, January 9	1109	1697, July 20	1191	1777, February 9	1274	1857, August 22
1027	1617, December 29	1110	1698, July 10	1192	1778, January 30	1275	1858, August 11
1028	1618, December 19	1111	1699, June 29	1193	1779, January 19	1276	1859, July 31
1029	1619, December 8	1112	1700, June 18	1194	1780, January 8*	1277	1860, July 20*
1030	1620, November 26*	1113	1701, June 8	1195	1780, December 28*	1278	1861, July 9
1031	1621, November 16	1114	1702, May 28	1196	1781, December 17	1279	1862, June 29
1032	1622, November 5	1115	1703, May 17	1197	1782, December 7	1280	1863, June 18
1033	1623, October 25	1116	1704, May 6*	1198	1783, November 26	1281	1864, June 6*
1034	1624, October 14*	1117	1705, April 25	1199	1784, November 14*	1282	1865, May 27
1035	1625, October 3	1118	1706, April 15	1200	1785, November 4	1283	1866, May 16
1036	1626, September 22	1119	1707, April 4	1201	1786, October 24	1284	1867, May 5
1037	1627, September 12	1120	1708, March 23*	1202	1787, October 13	1285	1868, April 24*
1038	1628, August 31*	1121	1709, March 18	1203	1788, October 2*	1286	1869, April 13
1039	1629, August 21			1204	1789, September 21	1287	1870, April 3

Solar Years

When later day astronomers discovered that the earth was not a fixed flat object but, instead, was a round revolving planet that orbited the sun every 365 days, 5 hours, and 49 minutes, they really upset the existing calendar systems of that time. As almost all ancient calendars were based on Lunar Years, mathematical conversion problems arose and still linger to haunt us.

As our modern calendar is based on 365 days, you can see that we are already 5 hours and 49 minutes shy of being a true Solar Year. To correct this error, we add an additional day every four years (leap year) and, as you can see, this is an over-correction of 11 minutes per year. Now, to take care of this built-in error, we leave out the leap year day, Feb. 29th, in each year that is divisible by 400 (1600 AD, 2000 AD, 2400 AD, etc.). All these errors and erroneous corrections makes it impossible to establish a hard-fast mathematical formula for converting Lunar Years to Solar Years.

Lunar Years

When early man first became interested in keeping track of time, it was long before clocks were invented. So, without better information, he turned to natural phenomenon that recurred at predictable times to act as his clock. The most obvious of these was the sun passing overhead each day. Even though they erroneously thought the sun rotated around a fixed earth, it was not too difficult for them to measure the transit time, from one day to the next, for the sun to reach a certain point in the sky. This was the first determination of a true day.

For measurements of longer periods of time, it was only logical that they used the moon for a clock. This bright object in the sky showed up as a new moon at regular intervals and its passage around the earth was used as a Lunar month. The next extension for time measurement was to recognize the fact that it was a certain number of moons from one season to the next — say from one harvest time to the next. This was the first establishment of a Lunar Year. As the moon actually orbits the earth in 29 days, 12 hours, 44 minutes and 2.8 seconds, the ancients were quite accurate when they used six 29 day months and six 30 day months for a Lunar Year — a total of 354 days.

CHANGING (AH) DATES TO (AD) DATES
General

Even though many countries have corrected their Lunar (AH) calendars to conform with the Solar (AD or SH) calendars, there are still many countries that stay with the old system. As a result, we must be able to change a Lunar (AH) coin date to a Solar (AD or SH) date to find the (AD) year the coin was minted. To do this, it is necessary to understand the following facts:

Lunar (AH) year = 354 days
Solar (SH) year = 365 days
Solar (AD) year = 365 days

Now, as Lunar (AH) years are shorter then (AD), or (SH), years, they pass by more quickly and the Lunar (AH) New Year will show up on an (AD) calendar approximately eleven days earlier in each succeeding (AD) year. Therefore, every (AD), or (SH), year contains portions of at least two (AH) years and, about every 32½ (AD) years, there can be one full (AH) year and parts of two others in one (AD), or (SH), year. You can see that a 354 day year would fit inside a 365 day year, with a little left over on each end. You can verify this by a close examination of the Hejira Date Chart D.

When actually converting a Lunar (AH) year to an (AD) year, you have two choices, as follows:

1) Look up the Lunar (AH) year on the excellent Hejira Date Chart D, and pay very close attention to the beginning date of that (AH) year.
2) Use the mathematical method of date conversion.

CHART E

HEJIRA DATE CHART

AH	AD	AH	AD	AH	AD	AH	AD
1288	1871, March 23	1319	1901, May 20	1350	1931, May 19	1381	1961, June 14
1289	1872, March 11*	1320	1902, April 10	1351	1932, May 7*	1382	1962, June 4
1290	1873, March 1	1321	1903, March 30	1352	1933, April 26	1383	1963, May 25
1291	1874, February 18	1322	1904, March 18*	1353	1934, April 16	1384	1964, May 13*
1292	1875, February 7	1323	1905, March 8	1354	1935, April 5	1385	1965, May 2
1293	1876, January 28*	1324	1906, February 25	1355	1936, March 24*	1386	1966, April 22
1294	1877, January 16	1325	1907, February 14	1356	1937, March 14	1387	1967, April 11
1295	1878, January 5	1326	1908, February 4*	1357	1938, March 3	1388	1968, May 31*
1296	1878, December 26	1327	1909, January 23	1358	1939, February 21	1389	1969, March 20
1297	1879, December 15	1328	1910, January 13	1359	1940, February 10*	1390	1970, March 9
1298	1880, December 4*	1329	1911, January 2	1360	1941, January 29	1391	1971, February 27
1299	1881, November 23	1330	1911, December 22	1361	1942, January 19	1392	1972, February 16*
1300	1882, November 12	1331	1912, December 11*	1362	1943, January 8	1393	1973, February 4
1301	1883, November 2	1332	1913, November 30	1363	1943, December 28	1394	1974, January 25
1302	1884, October 21*	1333	1914, November 19	1364	1944, December 17*	1395	1975, January 14
1303	1885, October 10	1334	1915, November 9	1365	1945, December 6	1396	1976, January 3*
1304	1886, September 30	1335	1916, October 28*	1366	1946, November 25	1397	1976, December 23*
1305	1887, September 19	1336	1917, October 17	1367	1947, November 15	1398	1977, December 12
1306	1888, September 7*	1337	1918, October 7	1368	1948, November 3*	1399	1978, December 2
1307	1889, August 28	1338	1919, September 26	1369	1949, October 24	1400	1979, November 21
1308	1890, August 17	1339	1920, September 15*	1370	1950, October 13	1401	1980, November 9*
1309	1891, August 7	1340	1921, September 4	1371	1951, October 2	1402	1981, October 30
1310	1892, July 26*	1341	1922, August 24	1372	1952, September 21*	1403	1982, October 19
1311	1893, July 15	1342	1923, August 14	1373	1953, September 10	1404	1983, October 8
1312	1894, July 5	1343	1924, August 2*	1374	1954, August 30	1405	1984, September 27*
1313	1895, June 24	1344	1925, July 22	1375	1955, August 20	1406	1985, September 16
1314	1896, June 12*	1345	1926, July 12	1376	1956, August 8*	1407	1986, September 6
1315	1897, June 2	1346	1927, July 1	1377	1957, July 29	1408	1987, August 26
1316	1898, May 22	1347	1928, July 20*	1378	1958, July 18	1409	1988, August 14*
1317	1899, May 12	1348	1929, July 9	1379	1959, July 7		
1318	1900, May 1	1349	1930, May 29	1380	1960, June 25*		

CHART F

TIBETAN CYCLICAL DATE CHART

13th Cycle 1747-1806 A.D.   15th Cycle 1867-1926 A.D.   17th Cycle 1987-2046 A.D.
14th Cycle 1807-1866 A.D.   16th Cycle 1927-1986 A.D.

Year	13	14	15	16	17	Year	13	14	15	16	17	Year	13	14	15	16	17
1	1747	1807	1867	1927	1987	21	1767	1827	1887	1947	2007	41	1787	1847	1907	1967	2027
2	1748	1808	1868	1928	1988	22	1768	1828	1888	1948	2008	42	1788	1848	1908	1968	2028
3	1749	1809	1869	1929	1989	23	1769	1829	1889	1949	2009	43	1789	1849	1909	1969	2029
4	1750	1810	1870	1930	1990	24	1770	1830	1890	1950	2010	44	1790	1850	1910	1970	2030
5	1751	1811	1871	1931	1991	25	1771	1831	1891	1951	2011	45	1791	1851	1911	1971	2031
6	1752	1812	1872	1932	1992	26	1772	1832	1892	1952	2012	46	1792	1852	1912	1972	2032
7	1753	1813	1873	1933	1993	27	1773	1833	1893	1953	2013	47	1793	1853	1913	1973	2033
8	1754	1814	1874	1934	1994	28	1774	1834	1894	1954	2014	48	1794	1854	1914	1974	2034
9	1755	1815	1875	1935	1995	29	1775	1835	1895	1955	2015	49	1795	1855	1915	1975	2035
10	1756	1816	1876	1936	1996	30	1776	1836	1896	1956	2016	50	1796	1856	1916	1976	2036
11	1757	1817	1877	1937	1997	31	1777	1837	1897	1957	2017	51	1797	1857	1917	1977	2037
12	1758	1818	1878	1938	1998	32	1778	1838	1898	1958	2018	52	1798	1858	1918	1978	2038
13	1759	1819	1879	1939	1999	33	1779	1839	1899	1959	2019	53	1799	1859	1919	1979	2039
14	1760	1820	1880	1940	2000	34	1780	1840	1900	1960	2020	54	1800	1860	1920	1980	2040
15	1761	1821	1881	1941	2001	35	1781	1841	1901	1961	2021	55	1801	1861	1921	1981	2041
16	1762	1822	1882	1942	2002	36	1782	1842	1902	1962	2022	56	1802	1862	1922	1982	2042
17	1763	1823	1883	1943	2003	37	1783	1843	1903	1963	2023	57	1803	1863	1923	1983	2043
18	1764	1824	1884	1944	2004	38	1784	1844	1904	1964	2024	58	1804	1864	1924	1984	2044
19	1765	1825	1885	1945	2005	39	1785	1845	1905	1965	2025	59	1805	1865	1925	1985	2045
20	1766	1826	1886	1946	2006	40	1786	1846	1906	1966	2026	60	1806	1866	1926	1986	2046

The Tibetan Cyclical Date system had its beginning in 966 A.D. The mathematics to change a Tibetan Cyclical date to an (AD) date is as follows: -

Cycle number x 60 years plus cycle 'yr' plus 966 = (AD) date

Mathematical Conversion

With only 354 days, Lunar (AH) years accumulate faster than Solar (SH) years so, in order to mathematically convert a Lunar (AH) date to an (AD) date, we must first correct the number of Lunar (AH) years in the date to the proper number of Solar (SH) years for the same time span. This is done as follows:

Lunar (AH) date -3.03% of Lunar (AH) date = Solar (SH) date

Before converting the Solar (SH) date to the proper (AD) date, it is necessary to know when the Solar (SH) dating system had its beginning.

(SH) Solar Hejira — This dating system had its beginning in 622 (AD), the same as the (AH) system, but the years accumulate at the rate of 365 days per year (except leap year).

After the Solar (SH) date has been determined, it is easy to convert to the proper (AD) date, as follows:

Solar (SH) date + 621 = (AD) date

Due to the overlapping of (AH) and (AD) years, and the fact that we have no way of knowing what part of an (AD) year the coin was minted, it is very easy to wind up with a one year error which is acceptable to most World Coin collectors.

Except for western (AD) dates, Arabic dates are the most widely used on World Coins. Just how did this come about? Well, the people of the western world often think that Columbus, Magellan, Balboa, and other great explorers, as being the real pioneers in discovering new lands. More than a thousand years prior to the time when Henry the Navigator, Queen Isabella I, and other western rulers sent off their brave Captains, the Arabs had already spread their influence across the north of Africa, down the east coast of Africa to the Cape, across southern Asia, into central Asia and on into the East Indies. It has been established that Arab traders had settlements on the northern coast of China, as far north as Tsingtao, in the fourth century (AD).

Good traders that they were, the Arabs soon originated trading values and this led to the use of money. As they were the prime-movers in this trade, it was their money that circulated. As a result of this extensive trading area, more than 100 countries have used Arabic dating on their coins.

On well struck coins, you will find that with a few hours practice you can locate and decipher the Arabic dates without referring to the chart. On poor quality coins, things will be different. You may find only 1, 2, or 3 digits of a 4 digit date; numbers will be tipped at every imagineable angle; and you will find portions of a date at one location on a coin and the remainder at a different location.

Various Date Types Found on Coins

(pd) Period Dating — There are certain coins with no dates (nd) that can be identified as being minted during a certain span of years. This is particularly true amongst the China/Empire cash coins with the square hole. If you refer to the listings of Emperors, at the beginning of the China section of your SCWC, you will be able to determine the Emperor who was in power and the dates of his reign. The reign dates will be the period date of the coin. The Chinese characters above and below the hole, on the obverse, will reveal the proper Emperor.

For Period Dating (pd) on early Japanese coins, refer to the section in this book, "DATES ON COINS OF JAPAN".

CHART G

THE CHINESE CALENDAR — TABLE

Year	Name	75th Cycle	76th Cycle A.D. DATES	77th Cycle	78th Cycle
1	Wood-Rat	1804	1864	1924	1984
2	Wood-Ox	1805	1865	1925	1985
3	Fire-Tiger	1806	1866	1926	1986
4	Fire-Hare	1807	1867	1927	1987
5	Earth-Dragon	1808	1868	1928	1988
6	Earth-Snake	1809	1869	1929	1989
7	Metal-Horse	1810	1870	1930	1990
8	Metal-Ram	1811	1871	1931	1991
9	Water-Monkey	1812	1872	1932	1992
10	Water-Cock	1813	1873	1933	1993
11	Wood-Dog	1814	1874	1934	1994
12	Wood-Boar	1815	1875	1935	1995
13	Fire-Rat	1816	1876	1936	1996
14	Fire-Ox	1817	1877	1937	1997
15	Earth-Tiger	1818	1878	1938	1998
16	Earth-Hare	1819	1879	1939	1999
17	Metal-Dragon	1820	1880	1940	2000
18	Metal-Snake	1821	1881	1941	2001
19	Water-Horse	1822	1882	1942	2002
20	Water-Ram	1823	1883	1943	2003
21	Wood-Monkey	1824	1884	1944	2004
22	Wood-Cock	1825	1885	1945	2005
23	Fire-Dog	1826	1886	1946	2006
24	Fire-Boar	1827	1887	1947	2007
25	Earth-Rat	1828	1888	1948	2008
26	Earth-Ox	1829	1889	1949	2009
27	Metal-Tiger	1830	1890	1950	2010
28	Metal-Hare	1831	1891	1951	2011
29	Water-Dragon	1832	1892	1952	2012
30	Water-Snake	1833	1893	1953	2013
31	Wood-Horse	1834	1894	1954	2014
32	Wood-Ram	1835	1895	1955	2015
33	Fire-Monkey	1836	1896	1956	2016
34	Fire-Cock	1837	1897	1957	2017
35	Earth-Dog	1838	1898	1958	2018
36	Earth-Boar	1839	1899	1959	2019
37	Metal-Rat	1840	1900	1960	2020
38	Metal-Ox	1841	1901	1961	2021
39	Water-Tiger	1842	1902	1962	2022
40	Water-Hare	1843	1903	1963	2023
41	Wood-Dragon	1844	1904	1964	2024
42	Wood-Snake	1845	1905	1965	2025
43	Fire-Horse	1846	1906	1966	2026
44	Fire-Ram	1847	1907	1967	2027
45	Earth-Monkey	1848	1908	1968	2028
46	Earth-Cock	1849	1909	1969	2029
47	Metal-Dog	1850	1910	1970	2030
48	Metal-Boar	1851	1911	1971	2031
49	Water-Rat	1852	1912	1972	2032
50	Water-Ox	1853	1913	1973	2033
51	Wood-Tiger	1854	1914	1974	2034
52	Wood-Hare	1855	1915	1975	2035
53	Fire-Dragon	1856	1916	1976	2036
54	Fire-Snake	1857	1917	1977	2037
55	Earth-Horse	1858	1918	1978	2038
56	Earth-Ram	1859	1919	1979	2039
57	Metal-Monkey	1860	1920	1980	2040
58	Metal-Cock	1861	1921	1981	2041
59	Water-Dog	1862	1922	1982	2042
60	Water-Boar	1863	1923	1983	2043

THE CHINESE CALENDAR CHART

(Cyclical Dates beginning with first year of cycle)

76th Cycle 1864-1923 A.D.
77th Cycle 1924-1983 A.D.
78th Cycle 1984-2043 A.D.

0 = Year in Cycle

CELESTIAL STEMS

TERRESTRIAL BRANCHES	甲 Wood	乙 Wood	丙 Fire	丁 Fire	戊 Earth	己 Earth	庚 Metal	辛 Metal	壬 Water	癸 Water
Rat 子	1 1864 1924 1984		13 1876 1936 1996		25 1888 1948 2008		37 1900 1960 2020		49 1912 1972 2032	
Ox 丑		2 1865 1925 1985		14 1877 1937 1997		26 1889 1949 2009		38 1901 1961 2021		50 1903 1973 2033
Tiger 寅	51 1914 1974 2034		3 1866 1926 1986		15 1878 1938 1998		27 1890 1950 2010		39 1902 1962 2022	
Hare 卯		52 1915 1975 2035		4 1867 1927 1987		16 1879 1939 1999		28 1891 1951 2011		40 1903 1963 2023
Dragon 辰	41 1904 1964 2024		53 1916 1976 2036		5 1868 1928 1988		17 1880 1940 2000		29 1892 1952 2012	
Snake 巳		42 1905 1965 2025		54 1917 1977 2037		6 1869 1929 1989		18 1881 1941 2001		30 1893 1953 2013
Horse 午	31 1894 1954 2014		43 1906 1966 2026		55 1918 1978 2038		7 1870 1930 1990		19 1882 1942 2002	
Ram 未		32 1895 1955 2015		44 1907 1967 2027		56 1919 1979 2039		8 1871 1931 1991		20 1883 1943 2003
Monkey 申	21 1884 1944 2004		33 1896 1956 2016		45 1908 1968 2028		57 1920 1980 2040		9 1872 1932 1992	
Cock 酉		22 1885 1945 2005		34 1897 1957 2017		46 1909 1969 2029		58 1921 1981 2041		10 1873 1933 1993
Dog 戌	11 1874 1934 1994		23 1886 1946 2006		35 1898 1958 2018		47 1910 1970 2030		59 1922 1982 2042	
Boar 亥		12 1875 1935 1995		24 1887 1947 2007		36 1899 1959 2019		48 1911 1971 2031		60 1923 1983 2043

The old Chinese Cyclical Date Calendar had its beginning in 2967 B.C. The mathematics to change a Cyclical Date to an (AD) date is as follows:

(Cycle number x 60 years) plus cycle year -2697 = (AD) date

DATING OF WORLD COINS
SECTION II

DATES ON COINS OF ARABIC INFLUENCED COUNTRIES

The Dating Systems used are as follows:

(AH) Mohammedan Era — This is a Lunar year system and is in accordance with the Islamic calendar. Its beginning was in 622 (AD) and is, by far, the most used dating on Arabic coins.

Calculations for (AH) Dating

Lunar (AH) date   -3.03% Lunar (AH) date = Solar (SH) date

Solar (SH) date   + 621 = (AD) date

(SH) Solar Hejira — This is a Solar year system and is mostly in Iran and Afghanistan. It had its beginning in 622 (AD), the same as the (AH) system, but years are added according to the Solar year (365 days), and not the Lunar year (354 days).

Calculations for (SH) Dating

Solar (SH) date   + 621 = (AD) date

(YR) Year of Reign — This is a system where coins are dated according to the reign of some emperor, king or ruler. The year, or part of a year, when the ruler assumed power is called the Accession year, and is 'yr' 1 of the reign. The 'yr' number found on the coin denotes the year during the reign when the coin was minted.

Calculations for (YR) Dating

Accession date (AD)   + 'yr' -1 = (AD) date

The Dating Systems used are as follows:

(dt) Direct Translation — This is where the date on the coin is displayed in Arabic numerals but it translates directly to the correct (AD) year the coin was minted.

(md) Multiple dates — Many Arabic coins have more than one dating system displayed on the same coin. Amongst the various countries, it is possible to find from one to three dating systems. Sometimes, the date numbers may be displayed in western, or other non-Arabic numeral systems.

(wa) Western to Arabic — With this system, the (AH) dates on coins are shown in western numerals. It is used almost exclusively to date Moroccan coins. The dates on the coins, even though displayed in western numerals, must be treated the same as any other (AH) date when changing it to an (AD) date.

(nd) No Date — Many Arabic coins have no dates displayed.

Refer to pages: 7-15, 17

0	½	1	2	3	4	5	6	7	8	9	10	50	100	500	1000
•	١/٢	١	٢	٣	٤	٥	٦	٧	٨	٩	١•	٥•	١••	٥••	١•••

EGYPT, 40 Para, Y-4

The 'yr' number on this coin translates to 10. The Accession date on this coin translates to 1277, which is a Lunar (AH) year.

Accession date	+ 'yr' -1 =	(AH) Mint year of coin
1277 (AH)	+ 10 -1 =	1286 (AH)
Lunar date	- 3.03% Lunar =	Solar date
1286	- 38 =	1248 (SH)
Date (SH)	+ 621 =	Date (AD)
1248	+ 621 =	1869 (AD)

From the Hejira Date Chart D, 1286 (AH) indicates 1869 (AD).

EGYPT, 20 Guerche, Y-22a

The 'yr' number on this coin translates to 5. The Accession date on this coin translates to 1293, which is a Lunar (AH) year.

Accession date	+ 'yr' -1 =	(AH) Mint year of coin
1293 (AH)	+ 5 -1 =	1297 (AH)
Lunar date	- 3.03% =	Solar Date
1297	- 39 =	1258 (SH)
Date (SH)	+ 621 =	Date (AD)
1258	+ 621 =	1879 (AD)

From the Hejira Date Chart D, 1297 (AH) indicates 1879 (AD).

23

ARABIC INFLUENCED COUNTRIES
YEAR OF REIGN
TURKISH ARABIC

Refer to pages: 7-15, 17

0	½	1	2	3	4	5	6	7	8	9	10	50	100	500	1000
•	١/٢	١	٢	٣	٤	٥	٦	٧	٨	٩	١٠	٥٠	١٠٠	٥٠٠	١٠٠٠

TURKEY, 100 Para, C-200a

The 'yr' number on this coin translates to 25.
The Accession date on this coin translates to
1223, which is a Lunar (AH) year.

Accession date	+ 'yr' -1 = (AH) Mint year of coin
1223 (AH)	+ 25 -1 = 1247 (AH)
Lunar date	-3.03% Lunar = Solar date
1247	-37 = 1210 (SH)
Date (SH)	+ 621 = Date (AD)
1210	+ 621 = 1831 (AD)

From the Hejira Date Chart D, 1247 (AH) indicates 1831 (AD).

TURKEY, 500 Piastres, Y-E51

The 'yr' number on this coin translates to 4.
The Accession date on this coin translates to
1327, which is a Lunar (AH) year.

Accession date	+ 'yr' -1 = (AH) Mint year of coin
1327 (AH)	+ 4 -1 = 1330 (AH)
Lunar date	-3.03% Lunar = Solar date
1330	-40 = 1290 (SH)
Date (SH)	+ 621 = Date (AD)
1290	+ 621 = 1911 (AD)

From the Hejira Date Chart D, 1330 (AH) indicates 1911 (AD).

Refer to pages: 5, 14, 17

0	½	1	2	3	4	5	6	7	8	9	10	50	100	500	1000
٥	١/٢	١	٢	٣	٤	٥	٤	‹	٨	٩	١٥	٥٥	١٥٥	٥٥٥	١٥٥٥

HYDERABAD/INDIA, Rupee, Y-17

The date number on this coin translates to 1317, which is a Lunar (AH) date.
From the Hejira Date Chart D, 1317 (AH) indicates 1899 (AD).

Lunar date	-3.03% Lunar = Solar date
1317	-40 = 1277 (SH)
Date (SH)	+ 621 = Date (AD)
1277	+ 621 = 1888 (AD) acceptable

HYDERABAD/INDIA, Rupee, C-48a

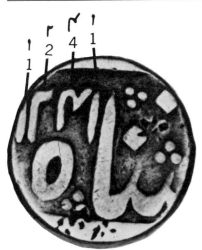

The date number on this coin translates to 1241, which is a Lunar (AH) date.
From the Hejira Date Chart D, 1241 (AH) indicates 1825 (AD).

Lunar date	-3.03% Lunar = Solar Date
1241	-37 = 1204 (SH)
Date (SH)	+ 621 = Date (AD)
1204	+ 621 = 1825 (AD)

ARABIC INFLUENCED COUNTRIES
(AH) MOHAMMEDAN ERA
PERSIAN ARABIC

Refer to pages: 5, 14, 17

0	½	1	2	3	4	5	6	7	8	9	10	50	100	500	1000
•	۱/۲	۱	۲	۳	۴	۵	۶ or ۶	۷	۸	۹	۱۰	۵۰	۱۰۰	۵۰۰	۱۰۰۰

IRAN, 2000 Dinars, Y-72

The date number on this coin translates to 1343, which is a Lunar (AH) date.
From the Hejira Date Chart D, 1334 (AH) indicates 1915 (AD).

Lunar date	-3.03% Lunar = Solar date
1334	-40 = 1294 (SH)
Date (SH)	+ 621 = Date (AD)
1294	+ 621 = 1915 (AD) acceptable

1 3 3 4
۱ ۳ ۳ ۴

IRAN, 2000 Dinars, Y-102

The date number on this coin translates to 1305, which is a Lunar (AH) date.
From the Hejira Date Chart D, 1305 (AH) indicates 1887 (AD).

Lunar date	-3.03% Lunar = Solar date
1305	-39 = 1266 (SH)
Date (SH)	+ 621 = Date (AD)
1266	+ 621 = 1887 (AD)

1 3 0 5
۱ ۳ ۰ ۵

Refer to pages: 5, 14, 17

0	½	1	2	3	4	5	6	7	8	9	10	50	100	500	1000
•	١/٢	١	٢	٣	٤	٥	٦	٧	٨	٩	١•	٥•	١••	٥••	١•••

SAUDI ARABIA, Ghirsh, Y-5

1 3 4 4
١ ٣ ٤ ٤

The date number on this coin translates to 1344, which is a Lunar (AH) date.
From the Hejira Date Chart D, 1344 (AH) indicates 1925 (AD).

Lunar date	-3.03% Lunar = Solar date
1344	-40 = 1304 (SH)
Date (SH)	+ 621 = Date (AD)
1304	+ 621 = 1925 (AD)

SAUDI ARABIA, ¼ Ghirsh, Y-9

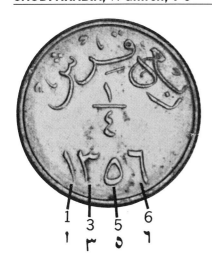

1 3 5 6
١ ٣ ٥ ٦

The date number on this coin translates to 1356, which is a Lunar (AH) date.
From the Hejira Date Chart D, 1356 (AH) indicates 1937 (AD).

Lunar date	-3.03% Lunar = Solar date
1356	-41 = 1315 (SH)
Date (SH)	+ 621 = Date (AD)
1315	+ 621 = 1936 (AD) acceptable

IRAN/Afghanistan
(SH) SOLAR HEJIRA
ARABIC

Refer to pages: 5, 10, 17

0	½	1	2	3	4	5	6	7	8	9	10	50	100	500	1000
•	۱⁄۲	۱	۲	۳	۴	۵	۶ or ۶	۷	۸	۹	۱۰	۵۰	۱۰۰	۵۰۰	۱۰۰۰

IRAN, 10 Rials, Y-149

The date number on this coin translates to 1340, which is a Solar (SH) date.

Date (SH)	+ 621 = Date (AD)
1346	+ 621 = 1967 (AD)

1 3 4 6
۱ ۳ ۴ ۶

AFGHANISTAN, 5 Amani, Y-51.2

The date number on this coin translates to 1299, which is a Solar (SH) date.

Date (SH)	+ 621 = Date (AD)
1299	+ 621 = 1920 (AD)

1 2 9 9
۱ ۲ ۹ ۹

Refer to page: 15

0	½	1	2	3	4	5	6	7	8	9	10	50	100	500	1000
•	١/r	١	٢	٣	٤	٥	٦ or ٦	٧	٨	٩	١•	٥•	١••	٥••	١•••

KUTCH, 1½ Dokda, Y-48

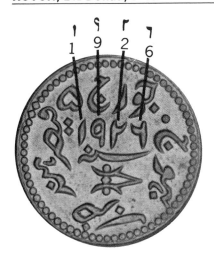

The date number on this coin translates to 1926.

Date (dt)	= Date (AD)
1926	= 1926 (AD)

Note: This coin would make a good example of multiple dating (md) as the reverse side has an excellent display of Kutch numerals for the (VS) date.

KUTCH, 2½ Kori, Y-52

The date number on this coin translates to 1917.

Date (dt)	= Date (AD)
1917	= 1917 (AD)

Note: This coin would make a good example of multiple dating as the reverse side has an excellent display of Kutch numerals for the (VS) date.

ARABIC INFLUENCED COUNTRIES
(md) MULTIPLE DATING

Refer to page: 15

0	½	1	2	3	4	5	6	7	8	9	10	50	100	500	1000
•	١/٢	١	٢	٣	۴	۵	٦ or ٧	٧	٨	٩	١٠	۵٠	١٠٠	۵٠٠	١٠٠٠

AFGHANISTAN, 5 Afghani, Y-102

The dates on this coin translates to 1340, which is a Solar (SH) date, and 1381, which is a Lunar (AH) date.
From the Conversion Table "Various Dating Systems to Date (AD)", 1340 (SH) indicates 1961 (AD). From the Hejira Date Chart D, 1381 (AD). See pages 23 to 28.

Lunar date	-3.03% Lunar = Solar date
1381 (AH)	-41 = 1340 (SH)
Date (SH)	+ 621 = Date (AD)
1340	+ 621 = 1961 (AD)

1340 (SH)   1381 (AH)
١٣۴٠   ١٣٨١

Refer to pages: 14, 15, 17

0	½	1	2	3	4	5	6	7	8	9	10	50	100	500	1000
•	١/٢	١	٢	٣	٤	٥	٦	٧	٨	٩	١٠	٥٠	١٠٠	٥٠٠	١٠٠٠

MAURITANIA, 5 Ouguiya, Y-3

The Arabic date on this coin translates to 1393, which is a Lunar (AH) date.
From the Hejira Date Chart D, 1393 (AH) indicates 1973 (AD).

Lunar date	-3.03% Lunar = Solar date
1393 (AH)	-42 = 1351 (SH)

From the Conversion Table, "Various Dating Systems to Date (AD)", 1351 (SH) = 1972 (AD). This is acceptable.

Date (SH)	+ 621 = Date (AD)
1351	+ 621 = 1972 (AD) acceptable

1 3 9 3
١ ٣ ٩ ٣

Refer to pages: 10, 14, 15, 17

0	½	1	2	3	4	5	6	7	8	9	10	50	100	500	1000

MOROCCO, 5 Mazunas, Y-2

1 3 1 0

The date on this coin, in western numerals, is 1310, which is a Lunar (AH) date.
From the Hejira Date Chart D, 1310 (AH) indicates 1892 (AD).

Lunar date	-3.03% Lunar = Solar date
1310 (AH)	-39 = 1271 (SH)
Date (SH)	+ 621 = Date (AD)
1271	+ 621 = 1892 (AD)

MOROCCO, 50 Francs, Y-51

1 3 7 1

The date number on this coin, in western numerals is 1371, which is a Lunar (AH) date.
From the Hejira Date Chart D, 1371 (AH) indicates 1950 (AD).

Lunar date	-3.03% Lunar = Solar date
1371 (AH)	-42 = 1329 (SH)
Date (SH)	+ 621 = Date (AD)
1329	+ 621 = 1950 (AD)

BANGLADESH
(dt) DIRECT TRANSLATION
BENGALI

DATES ON COINS OF BANGLADESH

The Dating System used is as follows:

(dt) Direct Translation — The coins of Bangladesh are dated according to the (dt) system and they will be displayed in Bengali numerals.

Calculations for (dt) Dating

Date (dt)   = Date (AD)

Refer to page: 15

0	½	1	2	3	4	5	6	7	8	9	10	50	100	500	1000
০	১⁄২	১	২	৩	৪	৫	৬	৭	৮	৯	১০	৫০	১০০	৫০০	১০০০

BANGLADESH, 5 Poisha, Y-9

The date number on this coin translates to 1977.

Date (dt)   = Date (AD)
1977   = 1977 (AD)

1 9 7 7
১ ৯ ৭ ৭

BANGLADESH, 10 Poisha, Y-6

১ ৯ ৭ ৮
1 9 7 4

The date number on this coin translates to 1974.

Date (dt)   = Date (AD)
1974   = 1974 (AD)

DATES ON COINS OF BHUTAN

The Dating Systems used are as follows:

(AD) Christian Era — Since 1957, Bhutan has been dating their coins according to this system.

~~(CD) Cyclical D~~ is evidence of a few coins of Bhutan being dated Dating system. Two examples are listed below:

■ *In comparing your reference catalogs I noticed a conflict between a listing in the **Standard Catalog of World Coins** and your **Illustrated Coin Dating Guide.** The photos for the cyclical dates of Bhutan are reversed in one of the two, but which one?*

The photos in question are of the cyclical dates used by Bhutan for the two varieties of the half rupee, struck with the Earth-Dragon (1928) or the Iron-Tiger (1950) cyclical dates. The Krause catalog department tells me that the photos are correct in the *Standard Catalog* and are reversed in the *Illustrated Coin Dating Guide.* To add a little confusion, the Earth-Dragon (1928) coin varieties were struck in 1929, 1930 and 1951. The Iron-Tiger (1950) pieces weren't struck until 1955.

1929 Year of Earth-Dragon

ཅ་ན་ཊ་སྨ།
ར་ཙ་དཥ།

BHUTAN, ½ Rupee, Y-4a/4b

1950 Year of Iron (Metal)-Tiger

Year of Iron (Metal)-Tiger

ཐ། ས་ང་ཋུག

BURMA
(CS) CHULA-SAKARAT ERA
BURMESE

DATE ON COINS OF BURMA

The Dating Sytems used are as follows:

(CS) Chula-Sakarat Era — The coins of Burma, prior to the Republic, were dated according to this system. The Chula-Sakarat Era Dating system had its beginning in 638 (AD).

Calculations for (CS) Dating

Date (CS)   + 638 = Date (AD)

(dt) Direct Translation — The Burmese Republic coins, since their independence in 1948, have been dated in Burmese numerals which translate directly to the correct (AD) date.

Calculations for (dt) Dating

Date (dt)   = Date (AD)

Refer to pages: 5, 10

0	½	1	2	3	4	5	6	7	8	9	10	50	100	500	1000
o	⅔	၁	၂	၃	၄	၅	၆	၇	၈	၉	၁၀	၅၀	၁၀၀	၅၀၀	၁၀၀၀

BURMA, Kyat, Y-7

The date number on this coin translates to 1214.

Date (CS)   + 638 = Date (AD)
1214   + 638 = 1852 (AD)

1   2   1   4
၁   ၂   ၁   ၄

34

Refer to page: 15

0	½	1	2	3	4	5	6	7	8	9	10	50	100	500	1000
၀	၃/၄	၁	၂	၃	၄	၅	၆	၇	၈	၉	၁၀	၅၀	၁၀၀	၅၀၀	၁၀၀၀

BURMA, 2 Mu 1 Pe, Y-8

The date number on this coin translates to 1228.

Date (CS)	+ 638 = Date (AD)
1228	+ 638 = 1866 (AD)

1 2 2 8
၁ ၂ ၂ ၈

BURMA, 50 Pyas, Y-22

The date number on this coin translates to 1952.

Date (dt)	= Date (AD)
1952	= 1952 (AD)

1 9 5 2
၁ ၉ ၅ ၂

35

BURMA
(dt) DIRECT TRANSLATION
BURMESE

Refer to page: 15

0	½	1	2	3	4	5	6	7	8	9	10	50	100	500	1000
o	⅔	၁	J	၃	၄	၅	၆	၇	၈	၉	၁၀	၅၀	၁၀၀	၅၀၀	၁၀၀၀

BURMA, Kyat, Y-23

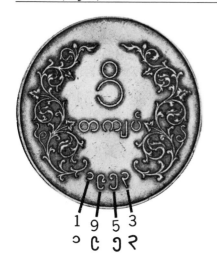

The date number on this coin translates to 1953.

Date (dt)	= Date (AD)
1953	= 1953 (AD)

1 9 5 3

CHINA
The People and Their Money

Only a few years ago, China presented the curious spectacle of an Empire without gold or silver currency in general use. For centuries the cash piece, with a square hole in the center for convenience in stringing, had been the medium of exchange. It had a raised broad rim, and a raised rim around the square hole at the center. In the sunken areas between these rims, on the obverse of the coins, are four raised characters. The top and bottom characters are the Emperor's Reign title and the right and left meant 'current coin'. Many of the coins also have two Manchu characters on the reverse meaning the 'mint', and the other meaning 'currency'. For centuries before Christ until about World War II, these were the circulating coins of China.

There were a few attempts in the past to coin silver. The Arabian traders brought to China the use of silver by weight, and the European traders at a later period brought the 8 Reales, Peso or Dollar. In the past, the copper cash was originally worth 1/1000 of a silver tael and the tael was divided into 10 mace, a mace into 10 candareens, and the candareen into 10 li. There was, however, very little tael coinage in existence. The tael is a unit of weight, not a coin, and generally being about 1⅓ ounces of silver. In 1936, the Nanking Government officially abolished the tael as a monetary value and gradually all financial expressions changed to dollars and cents, with the official Chinese name being 'Yuan'.

The Chinese cash had the distinction of being a symbol of prosperity and was popular to the point of being worn as an amulet or ornament. One cash coin, produced about 206 B.C. and having a value of 5/24th of a tael, was considered to be both lucky and decorative. Similar pieces were hung around the neck on a chain or cord, and were reproduced in gold, silver, bronze, and jade. Genuine coins of this type are, however, extremely rare. Cash coins of a later period strung on a string in such an order that the characters on the coins formed a rhyme, were believed to have great talismanic powers. A few cash coins strung on a red string, hung for a short time around the neck of a city god, were believed to acquire great virtue and, when worn by children, would repel evil influences. Strings of cash hung on a child's neck, the number being equal to the age of the child, a fresh coin being added every year until the age of 15, was believed to be able to assist the child in passing the 30 dangerous barriers which they meet in the first 15 years of life.

Many different materials served as currency in times past. We may mention skins, tortoise shells, cowries, axe heads, spades, amulets, rings, silk rolls, paper, gold, silver, tea bricks, copper, brass, zinc, and iron. Copper coinage has existed for more than 25 centuries. In 1032 AD, currency regulations were established which said that metal pieces would henceforth be exchanged according to their weight. This was the first standard exchange method between the various metal sizes used as currency.

The round copper (also brass, bronze, zinc and iron) cash coin is symbolic of 'heaven' (formerly believed to be round), and the square hole is symbolic of 'earth' (formerly believed to be square). The copper coins strung on a string in lots of 100 or 1000 (depending on which area of China) were used to make larger purchases without counting each coin.

Because copper coins were heavy and difficult to transport in quantities, it was normal that good business men, which the Chinese certainly were, early invented the bank note. It seems that Chinese merchants were using bank notes about 800 AD. There is an actual specimen written about 1370 AD in the British Museum. It is about the size of foolscap paper, and is almost black. Each money shop (the forerunners to banks) had its own paper with a particular ornamental border and other easily recognized features. Few counterfeit notes were in existence owing to the limited range of the notes and because the notes were most often redeemed at the shop of issue. Marco Polo, in his visit to China, described Kublai Khan making many purchases paying for it with money which he himself wrote. If any of these 'personal checks' became damaged, the owner could get a new one written by paying 3% of its face value. It is estimated that this Mongol ruler in 34 years issued more than $624,000,000 worth of paper money. This also leads to the speculation that the Great Khan may have been a better money manipulator than a soldier. Subsequent Mongol Emperors added fuel to the flame of discontent that the Chinese had for the Mongols. Worthless checks had much to do with the uprising and the establishment of the Chinese Ming Dynasty.

Cash pieces are undated coins that must be identified by the characters indicating the reigning Emperor, the place of mintage, and other slight variations. Too, all but the most recent are cast coins, made by pouring molten metal into a mold. A cast coin can sometimes be identified by dropping it on a hard surface. The casting process seems to make the coin harder than those that are struck and the ringing sound is of a much higher pitch. The cash coins shown in SCWC obviously are only a small portion of the untold millions that have been minted through the ages. The best method of identifying such coins is to try to discern the Emperor, province or political subdivision where the coin was minted, the numbers, and other characters shown. As a last resort, go page-by-page in the SCWC and compare your coin to the nearest resemblance shown. If you have very many, you surely won't be able to pin them all down.

At one time, the cash piece was a fairly valuable coin of trade, as far as the average Chinese were concerned. Later, especially after 1900 when many foreigners came to China, this coin became so devaluated that it merely served as 'coolie' money. For example: It took 1000 cash pieces to equal one Yuan and before the U.S. went off the Gold Standard (1933), the exchange rate was $5.25 (Yuan) for $1.00 (U.S.) — this made it 5250 cash pieces for one U.S. Dollar, or 52½ cash pieces per U.S. cent. After the U.S. abandoned the Gold Standard, the exchange dropped to $3.25 (Yuan) to $1.00 (U.S.) — or 32½ cash pieces per U.S. cent. During these same years, a Chinese dockworker might carry 100 lb. sacks of grain off the dock and into a large godown (warehouse) where it was stacked — sometimes a distance of six or eight hundred feet. For each sack carried, the coolie would receive a 'clacker' (cash piece). This means the worked must carry from thirty to fifty sacks to earn the equivalent of one U.S. cent. About February 1, 1936, the Government Central Mint began issuing the first National Currency of China. The new coins were 20¢, 10¢, and 5¢ made of nickel — also 1¢ and ½¢ made of copper (bronze). Pure nickel is magnetic, is very hard and only by use of excellent machinery, can the lines on the coins be clear and sharp. The coins had a distinctive lustre and nickel does not tarnish. Because of these facts, it was thought that the nickel coin would be hard to counterfeit. Newspaper reports said that within two days after the new coins were distributed by the Central Bank, counterfeit nickels were found in circulation. They, however, were very crude and easy to detect.

The Chinese and counterfeiting seem to be as compatible as pie and ice cream. From 1900 until World War II, copying and altering coins and paper currency nearly became the second most popular pastime in China. Nearly all types of precious and semi-precious metal coins in circulation were counterfeited or devalued in one way or another. Coins were shaved, and clipped; cut apart edgeways and some of the metal scooped out and replaced with base metal, and then rejoined; and then there were thousands of the completely faked coins. Paper money was worse than metal. Basically, there were three types of money in circulation; the good and accepted; that which had been issued by some bank that subsequently went out of business, making their paper money worthless; and the out-and-out counterfeit, which was usually noticed by the poor quality of paper used. Foreigners were the best marks for bad paper money. Most couldn't read Chinese character writing and had no knowledge of a good bank, or a bad one. One American resident of Shanghai stated, "It seems that everyone in China waits for me to come along so they can pass off their bogus money. I guess you're 'sposed to pass it off on someone more stupid but I have trouble finding such people. Instead, I just throw it in a drawer and look at it, from time to time, to convince myself that I'm not so smart, after all."

The Chinese people, like those of many other countries, were very suspicious of banks. In the past, they had been bitten so many times by worthless paper money, of one kind or another, that they learned to place their faith only in good quality coins. The more pure the gold or silver in a coin, the more readily it was accepted. This led to wide circulation within China of superior quality foreign coins.

Many countries soon recognized the fact that a good coin could give them an advantage in the China trade. As a result, Spanish Colonial 8 Reales, Mexican pesos, Japanese, British, and American Trade dollars, French/Saigon piastres, and the silver Japanese yen, at various times had the upper hand in trade. The most popular of all was the Mexican peso and it was estimated that some 550 million were circulated in China. So many, in fact, that the Chinese money gained the word 'Mex' as a nickname.

The first Chinese minted dollar that was widely accepted was the high silver content Yuan Shih K'ai dollar, first minted in 1914. Even as late as the middle 1930's, the paper money from the coastal city of Amoy wasn't honored in other parts of China so anyone taking money out of that city was sure to leave with the bulky, but valuable, Shih K'ai's.

The best advice to a collector of Chinese coins is to have patience. At first, the strange characters on the coins seem impossible to decipher and people often give up on them. However, if you carefully read the reambles in SCWC, and study the photographs of the coins, you will soon begin to understand the systems used and to be able to find the Chinese characters that pertain to the date.

DATES ON COINS OF CHINA/Empire

The Dating Systems used are as follows:

(AH) Mohammedan Era — The far western Province of Sinkiang had many coins dated by the (AH) system. They will not be treated in this section, but will be included in the section, "Dates on Coins of the Arabic Influenced Countries".

(CD) Cyclical Dating — Many coins of the China/Empire were dated according to the 60 year recurring cycle method — (CD). Although the Empire had the central government mint, and many provincial mints, the method of dating and designing coins was well organized.

(YR) Year of Reign Dating — Chinese Empire

It seems that the earliest coins shown in the SCWC that is dated according to the (YR) Year of Reign system are from Kiangsu (Shanghai issue) and they indicate 'yr' 6 of the Hsien Feng reign (1851-1861 AD). So, for the following (YR) Year of Reign Table, it will begin with that Emperor.

(YR) Year of Reign — This is a dating system where coins are dated according to the reign of some emperor, king or ruler. The year, or part of a year, when the ruler assumed power is called the Accession Date, and is 'yr' 1 of the reign. The 'yr' is increased by one for each succeeding year that ruler is in power. This 'yr' number found on the coin also denotes the particular year during the reign when the coin was minted. The best way to establish the proper Accession date for a ruler is to look up the preamble to the Chinese section of your Standard Catalog of World Coins.

The mathematics to determine a (YR) date are as follows:

(YR) Year of Reign Dating

Accession date + 'yr' number on coin -1 = Date (AD)

(nd) No Date — Most of the coins of the China/Empire had no dates.

(YR) Year of Reign Dating Tables

Accession date (1851 AD)			Hsien Feng (1851-1861 AD)			Accession Date (1861 AD)		
'yr'	Chinese Year	AD Year	'yr'	Chinese Year	AD Year	Ch'i-hsiang (1861 AD)		
						'yr'	Chinese Year	AD Year
1	一	1851	7	七	1857			
2	二	1852	8	八	1858	1	一	1861
3	三	1853	9	九	1859			
4	四	1854	10	十	1860			
5	五	1855	11	一十	1861	As Emperor Ch'i-hsiang ruled only for a portion of one year and his Accession Date is 1861 (AD).		
6	六	1856						

CHINA/Empire
(YR) YEAR OF REIGN
DATING TABLE

Accession Date (1862 AD)   T'ung Chih (1862-1875 AD)

'yr'	Chinese Year	AD Year	'yr'	Chinese Year	AD Year
1	一	1862	8	八	1869
2	二	1863	9	九	1870
3	三	1864	10	十	1871
4	四	1865	11	一十	1872
5	五	1866	12	二十	1873
6	六	1867	13	三十	1874
7	七	1868	14	四十	1875

Formerly known as Ch'i-hsiang. Emperor T'ung-chih (1862-1875 AD) ruled for nearly fourteen years and there are no examples of (YR) dated coins for his reign. His Accession Date was 1862 (AD).

Accession Date (1875 AD)   Kuang Hsu (1875-1908 AD)

'yr'	Chinese Year	AD Year	'yr'	Chinese Year	AD Year	'yr'	Chinese Year	AD Year
1	一	1875	13	三十	1887	24	四十二	1898
2	二	1876	14	四十	1888	25	五十二	1899
3	三	1877	15	五十	1889	26	六十二	1900
4	四	1878	16	六十	1890	27	七十二	1901
5	五	1879	17	七十	1891	28	八十二	1902
6	六	1880	18	八十	1892	29	九十二	1903
7	七	1881	19	九十	1893	30	十三	1904
8	八	1882	20	十二	1894	31	一十三	1905
9	九	1883	21	一十二	1895	32	二十三	1906
10	十	1884	22	二十二	1896	33	三十三	1907
11	一十	1885	23	三十二	1897	34	四十三	1908
12	二十	1886						

The coins dated by the (YR) method during the Hsuan T'ung reign (1908-1911 AD) are confusing. There are coins showing that 'yr' 1 of the reign as 1909 and others indicating 'yr' 1 as 1910. Then, many coins showing 'yr' 3 as being 1911 are evident. Now, if 1908 was the Accession date, then 1911 would be 'yr' 4, not 'yr' 3. Because of these contradictions, we will assume 1909 as being the correct Accession date.

Accession Date (1909 AD)			Hsuan T'ung (1908-1911 AD)		
'yr'	Chinese Year	AD Year	'yr'	Chinese Year	AD Year
1	一	1909	3	三	1911
2	二	1910			

The few coins minted during the Hung Hsein reign (1915-1916 AD) are also confusing. As he declared himself Emperor in December 1915, and died in June 1916, it is possible that some mints may have considered 1916 as being the first year of his reign. There are coins showing both 1915 and 1916 as being 'yr' 1 of the Hung Hsein reign. For purposes of this Table, we will assume 1915 as being the correct Accession Date.

Accession Date (1915 AD)			Hung Hsein (1915-1916 AD)		
'yr'	Chinese Year	AD Year	'yr'	Chinese Year	AD Year
1	一	1915	2	二	1916

EMPERORS — Chinese Empire

KAO TSUNG 1736-1795

JEN TSUNG 1796-1820

Type A-1
Reign title: Ch'ien Lung
乾 隆 通 寶
Ch'ien-lung T'ung-pao

Type A-2
乾 隆 通 寶
Chien-shan-lung T'ung Pao

Type A
Reign title: Chia Ch'ing
嘉 慶 通 寶
Chia-ch'ing T'ung-pao

HSUAN TSUNG 1821-1851

Type A
Reign title: Tao Kuang
道 光 通 寶
Tao-kuang T'ung-pao

WEN TSUNG 1851-1861

Type A
Reign title: Hsien Feng
咸 豐 通 寶
Hsien-feng T'ung-pao

Type B-1
咸 豐 重 寶
Hsien-feng Chung-pao

Type B-2
咸 豐 重 寶
Hsien-feng Chung-pao

Type C
咸 豐 元 寶
Hsien-feng Yuan-pao

MU TSUNG 1861

Type A-1
1st reign title: Ch'i Hsiang
祺 祥 通 寶
Ch'i-hsiang T'ung-pao

MU TSUNG 1862-1875

Type B-1
祺 祥 重 寶
Ch'i-hsiang Chung-pao

Type A-2
2nd reign title: T'ung Chih
同 治 通 寶
T'ung-chih T'ung-pao

Type B-2
同 治 重 寶
T'ung-chih Chung-pao

42

TE TSUNG 1875-1908

| **Type A** | **Type B** | **Type C** |

Reign title: Kuang Hsu

光 緒 通 寶
Kuang-hsu T'ung-pao

光 緒 重 寶
Kuang-hsu Chung-pao

光 緒 元 寶
Kuang-hsu Yuan-pao

HSUAN T'UNG
Ti (Hsun Ti) 1908-1911

YUAN SHIH KAI
Dec. 15, 1915-March 21,
1916

Type A

Reign title: Hsuan T'ung

宣 統 通 寶
Hsuan-t'ung T'ung-pao

Reign title: Hung-Hsien

洪 憲 通 寶
Hung-hsien Tung-pao

CYCLICAL DATES
General

Time, in many of the ancient countries of the world, was measured in cycles of 60 year periods. These cycles of 60 years were recorded much like the westerners of today record centuries of 100 years. One explanation of the 60 years period is the most regular conjunction in the sky of two great planets — Jupiter and Saturn. Every 60 years, these two bodies meet again in almost the same place in the sky as seen from earth. This 60 year period is the famous 'soss' of the Chaldeans and is equal approximately to the 60 years cycle, or Chiatze, of the Chinese.

The Chinese, although they don't often get proper credit for their accomplishments, probably had astronomical skills that were equal to, or maybe exceeded, those of the Chaldeans, for the same period in time (600-800 BC). Even though fairly skilled in heavenly matters, the Chinese believed, as did all other cultures of the time, that the earth was a flat, fixed plane and was the center of the universe. In fact, even today in Peking there is a beautiful, raised stone platform, with elegant carved stone railings where the 'hub' stone of the polished circular paving is considered to be the very center of the universe. Who's to argue?

After the Chinese adopted the 60 years cycle system, they attached names so that individual years of the cycle could be easily determined. The system devised was 10 celestial stems which include two each of the following: Wood, Fire, Earth, Metal, and Water. These are combined with the 12 terrestrial branches which correspond to the Western sings of the Zodiac and are: Rat, Ox, Tiger, Hare, Dragon, Snake, Horse, Ram, Monkey, Cock, Dog, and Boar. Each year of the cycle is named by the combination of one stem and one branch. As there are 5 of one and 12 of the other, it is necessary to complete the 60 years before the same combination of Wood-Rat would occur again. Each year of the cycle has a Star God, who presides over those born in that particular year. The worshipper pays particular attention to the god of his year on each succeeding anniversary.

China adopted the Western (Gregorian) Calendar in November 1911 and since then they have officially recorded the years as, so many years of the Chinese Republic. In order to wean the Chinese people away from the old Cyclical Dating, the Government actually passed a law prohibiting the printing and distribution of the Old Calendar. However, in private life and in native business, the old customs sometimes prevail. Bootleg printing and selling of the Old Calendars still flourished up into the 1930's.

Today, the Cyclical Dating references found on recent coins is only a matter of nostalgia. The celestial-stem name has been dropped and only the names of the Zodiac animals are used. Such names as 'Year of the Dragon', 'Year of the Monkey', etc., now repeat every 12 years.

Note: Cyclical Dating will get more detailed treatment in the section, "Cyclical Dates on the Coins of China/Empire".

CHINA
Chinese Coin Dating by the Cyclical Dating (CD) Chart

Many Chinese Empire and Provincial issue coins were dated by the Cyclical Date (CD) method — this fact is evident by looking through the China section of your SCWC where many dates are preceded by the letters 'CD'. To convert these dates to the western dates (AD), is often difficult. The best aid for Cyclical dates is the chart, containing 120 squares, which is shown in the preambles to the China and Vietnam sections of SCWC. The main difficulty is to locate the proper characters on the coin that pertain to the date.

First, find a character on the coin that corresponds with a character shown at the top of the Cyclical Date Chart (CD). Then, do the same, only compare with the characters shown down the left side of the chart. After these two are determined, follow to where the two lines join and in that square is shown the western date (AD). Usually, but not always, the latest date shown is the date of the coin. In case of an older coin, the earlier date shown will probably be the correct one.

For practice, it is easy to pick a coin with a known date and a (CD) prefix from the page of SCWC. Then, the date that is shown below the picture (SCWC) is found on the Cyclical Date Chart (CD) and then copy the two pertinent Chinese characters (one from the top and one from the side) for that western date. The search is then on to find these two characters on the coin. If you repeat this learning lesson a few times, it will improve your ability to recognize a Cyclical Date character, and give you an insight to where they are located on various coins. They are not always side-by-side and, on some coins, one may be near the right edge and to other the left.

Now, everyone has heard of such terms as, "Year of the Rat", and "Year of the Dragon". These are from the Old Chinese Calendar, which is the 60 year recurring method of Cyclical Dating. If you take the Cyclical Date Chart, as shown in SCWC, you can determine dates using the proper terminology. Across the top of the Chart, beginning with the left vertical column, insert the words: Metal, Metal, Water, Water, Wood, Wood, Fire, Fire, and Earth, Earth. Down the left side, beginning at the top line, insert the words: Dog, Boar, Rat, Ox, Tiger, Hare, Dragon, Snake, Horse, Ram, Monkey, and Cock. Now, you have a Cyclical Date Chart using words instead of Chinese characters.

This word system doesn't help much in determining dates on Chinese coins, but is shown for its general interest. Although, in the Chinese section of your SCWC, you will find such coins as the 1916 Hung Hsien Dollar — Y-332. On this coin there is a Fire-Dragon. Now, if you use your worded Cyclical Date Chart, you will find the word "Fire" at the top of the 1916 column, and "Dragon" at the left of the 1916 line. Hence, 1916 is the year of the "Fire-Dragon".

Other coins of interest, related to the worded Cyclical Dating System, are the recent issues of Hong Kong. There are coins with the Dragon, Snake, Horse, Sheep (Ram), Monkey, and Cock shown. Using the Chinese Calendar Table, page 20, you will find that the animal on the coin corresponds to the proper Zodiac animal for that year. There is one Singapore coin, 10 Dollar — 1981 — Y-17a, that displays all the Cyclical date (Zodiac) animals on one coin.

Cyclical Date Chart

Although the Cyclical Date Charts shown in your SCWC and the one in this book, chart H, accomplish the same thing, we will use the one in this book as reference for all (CD) dating purposes. The reason for this is as follows:
1. The year span of the last three cycles are shown.
2. The proper word terminology is included so that you may become accustomed to the "Celestial Stem" and "Terrestrial Branches" of the system.
3. The Chart begins with the first year of a cycle.
4. In each dated square, there is a small box which contains the 'yr' number within a cycle.

Refer to pages: 5, 20, 21

ANHWEI, Dollar, Y-45.4

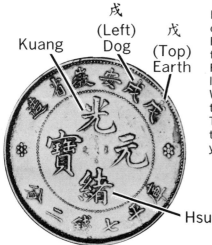

Kuang

(Left)
Dog

戊

戊
(Top)
Earth

Hsu

Refer to the Chinese Cyclical Date Chart on chart H.
Find the Chinese character for "Earth" at the top of the Cyclical Date Chart.
Find the Chinese character for "Dog" at the left side of the Cyclical Date Chart.
Where these two lines cross, the box contains the proper (AD) date.
The Chinese Calendar Table chart G, indicates the dates 1838, 1898, 1958 & 2018. From your SCWC, 1898 (AD) is the proper date.

FUKIEN, 2 Cash, Y-8f

午
(Left)
Horse

丙
(Top)
Fire

Refer to the Chinese Cyclical Date Chart on chart H.
Find the Chinese character for "Fire" at the top of the Cyclical Date Chart.
Find the Chinese character for "Horse" at the left side of the Cyclical Date Chart.
Where the two lines cross, the box contains the proper (AD) date.
The Chinese Calendar Table, chart G, indicates the dates 1846, 1906, 1966 & 2026. From your SCWC, 1906 (AD) is the proper date.

Refer to pages: 5, 20, 21

GENERAL ISSUE, Dollar, K-212

未
Ram
(Left)

丁
Fire
(Top)

Refer to the Chinese Cyclical Date Chart on chart H.
The Chinese Calendar Table, chart G, indicates the dates 1847, 1907, 1967 & 2027. From your SCWC, 1907 (AD) is the proper date.
Find the Chinese character for "Fire" at the top of the Cyclical Date Chart.
Find the Chinese character for "Ram" at the left side of the Cyclical Date Chart.
Where these two lines cross, the box contains the proper (AD) date.

GENERAL ISSUE, 10 Cash, Y-20x

Cock
(Left)
酉

Earth
(Top)
己

Refer to the Chinese Cyclical Date Chart on chart H.
Find the Chinese character for "Earth" at the top of the Cyclical Date Chart.
Find the Chinese character for "Cock" at the left side of the Cyclical Date Chart.
Where these two lines cross, the box contains the proper (AD) date.
The Chinese Calendar Table, chart G, indicates the dates 1849, 1909, 1969 & 2029. From your SCWC, 1909 (AD) is the proper date.

47

Refer to pages: 5, 18, 20

KIANGNAN, Dollar, Y-145a.10

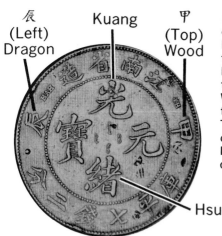

辰
(Left)
Dragon

Kuang

甲
(Top)
Wood

Hsu

Refer to the Chinese Cyclical Date Chart on chart H.
Find the Chinese character for "Wood" at the top of the Cyclical Date Chart.
Find the Chinese character for "Dragon" at the left side of the Cyclical Date Chart.
Where these two lines cross, the box contains the proper (AD) date.
The Chinese Calendar Table, chart G, indicates the dates 1844, 1904, 1964 & 2024. From your SCWC, 1904 (AD) is the proper date.

KIANGNAN, 20 Cents, Y-143a.6

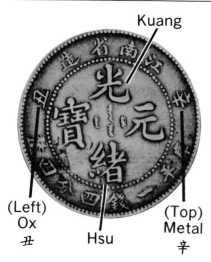

Kuang

(Left)
Ox
丑

Hsu

(Top)
Metal
辛

Refer to the Chinese Cyclical Date Chart on chart H.
Find the Chinese character for "Metal" at the top of the Cyclical Date Chart.
Find the Chinese character for "Ox" at the left side of the Cyclical Date Chart.
Where these two lines cross, the box contains the proper (AD) date.
The Chinese Calendar Table, chart G, indicates the dates 1841, 1901, 1961 & 2021. From your SCWC, 1901 (AD) is the proper date.

Refer to pages: 7-15

0	½	1	2	3	4	5	6	7	8	9	10	50	100	500	1000
零	半	一	二	三	四	五	六	七	八	九	十	十五	百	百五	千
		壹	貳	叁	肆	伍	陸	柒	捌	玖	拾	拾伍	佰	佰伍	仟

ANHWEI, Dollar, Y-45.2

The Chinese 'yr' number on this coin translates to 2, 10 and 4. To change this to a useable number, do as follows:

(2 x 10) + 4 = 24

Note: Read Chinese from R to L.

Accession date + 'yr' -1 = Date (AD)

1875   + 24 -1 + 1898 (AD)

This coin was minted during the Reign of Kuang Hsu (Te Tsung 1875-1908 AD). His Accession date is 1875 (AD).

ANHWEI, 50 Cents, Y-44

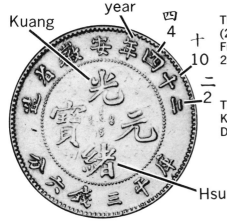

The 'yr' number on this coin translates to 24.

(2 x 10) + 4 = 24

From the 'yr' Conversion Table, page 40, 'yr' 24 indicates 1898 (AD).

Accession date + 'yr' -1 = Date (AD)

1875   + 24 -1 = 1898 (AD)

This coin was minted during the Reign of Kuang Hsu (1875-1908 AD). The Accession Date for Kuang Hsu was 1875 (AD).

CHINA/Empire
(YR) YEAR OF REIGN
CHINESE

Refer to pages: 7-15

0	½	1	2	3	4	5	6	7	8	9	10	50	100	500	1000
零	半	一	二	三	四	五	六	七	八	九	十	十五	百	百五	千
		壹	貳	叁	肆	伍	陸	柒	捌	玖	拾	拾伍	佰	佰伍	仟

CHIHLI, Dollar, Y-65

The Chinese 'yr' number on this coin translates to 2, 10 and 2. To change this to a useable number, do as follows:

(2 x 10) + 2 = 22

Note: Read Chinese R to L.

Accession date + 'yr' -1 = Date (AD)

1875 + 22 -1 = 1896 (AD)

This coin was minted during the Reign of Kuang Hsu (Te Tsung 1875-1908 AD). His Accession date is 1875 (AD).

EMPIRE, 10 Cash, Y-27

The 'yr' number on this coin translates to 3. From the 'yr' Conversion Table, page 41, 'yr' 3 indicates 1911.

Accession date + 'yr' -1 = Date (AD)

1909 + 3 -1 = 1911 (AD)

There is much confusion about the Reign of Hsuan T'ung. Although his Reign is listed as (1908-1911 AD), most coins of his Reign, however agree with his Accession Date as being 1909 (AD) and we will use that date for coin dating purposes.

Refer to pages: 7-15

0	½	1	2	3	4	5	6	7	8	9	10	50	100	500	1000
零	半	一	二	三	四	五	六	七	八	九	十	十五	百	百五	千
		壹	貳	叁	肆	伍	陸	柒	捌	玖	拾	拾伍	佰	佰伍	仟

KIANGSU, 5 Ch'ien, Y-910

Hsien
Feng

6 六

year

The 'yr' number on this coin translates to 6.
From the 'yr' Conversion Table, page 39, 'yr' 6
indicates 1856 (AD).

Accession date + 'yr' -1 = Date (AD)
1851 + 6 -1 = 1856 (AD)

This coin was minted during the Reign of Hsien
Feng (1851-1861 AD). The Accession Date for
Hsien Feng was 1851 (AD).

KWEICHOW, Dollar, K-9

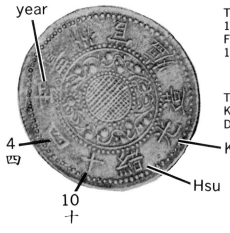

year

4
四

10
十

Kuang

Hsu

The 'yr' number on this coin translates to 14.
10 + 4 = 14
From the 'yr' Conversion Table, page 40, 'yr'
14 indicates 1888 (AD).

Accession date + 'yr' -1 = Date (AD)
1875 + 14 -1 = 1888 (AD)

This coin was minted during the Reign of
Kuang Hsu (1875-1908 AD). The Accession
Date for Kuang Hsu was 1875 (AD).

CHINA/Empire
(YR) YEAR OF REIGN
CHINESE

Refer to pages: 7-15

0	½	1	2	3	4	5	6	7	8	9	10	50	100	500	1000
零	半	一	二	三	四	五	六	七	八	九	十	十五	百	百五	千
		壹	貳	叄	肆	伍	陸	柒	捌	玖	拾	拾伍	佰	佰伍	仟

KWANGSI, 7 Ch'ien, K-916

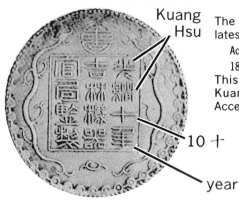

Kuang Hsu

10 十

year

The Chinese 'yr' number on this coin trans-lates to 10.

Accession date + 'yr' -1 = Date (AD)

1875   + 10 -1 = 1884 (AD)

This coin was minted during the Reign of Kuang Hsu (Te Tsung 1875-1908 AD). His Accession date is 1875 (AD).

MANCHURIAN, 20 Cents, Y-213

In English, 'First Year of Hsuan Tung''. Coin is listed as 1909 (AD) in the SCWC.
See note above.

DATES ON COINS OF CHINA/Republic (Mainland)

The Dating System used are as follows:

(CD) Cyclic Dating — There are a few coins of Kiangsu and Sinkiang which had (CD) dating even after the establishment of the Republic. These will not be treated separately in this section but, for further information, refer to, "Cyclical Dates on the Coins of China/Empire".

(YrRep) Year of Republic — The Republic had its beginning in 1912 (AD) and that is the Beginning Date of the Republic.

Calculations for (YrRep) Dating
Beginning of Republic + 'yr' 1- = Date (AD)

(YR) Year of Reign — There were a few coins dated with the (YR) system even after the establishment of the Republic. This happened when General Yuan Shih K'ai, because he had the biggest army in China, set himself up as Emperor, in 1915-1916 (AD). He died in 1916 and the empire ambitions along with him. In your SCWC, refer to the Hung Hsien Dollars, Y-332, Y-332a and Y-332b.

(nd) No Date — Many coins of the China/Republic (Mainland) have no dates.

Refer to pages: 15, 56

0	½	1	2	3	4	5	6	7	8	9	10	50	100	500	1000
零	半	一	二	三	四	五	六	七	八	九	十	十五	百	百五	千
		壹	貳	叁	肆	伍	陸	柒	捌	玖	拾	拾伍	佰	佰伍	仟

GENERAL ISSUE, Dollar, Y-329.6

Min Kuo Republic

The Chinese 'yr' number on this coin translates to 9.

From the 'yr'/Date (AD) Conversion Table, page 56, 'yr' 9 indicates 1920 (AD).

Beginning of
Republic   + 'yr' -1 = Date (AD)
1912   + 9 -1 = 1920 (AD)

Note: This is an example of a 'yr' number of one Chinese character.

CHINA/Republic (Mainland)
(YR REP YEAR OF REPUBLIC)
CHINESE

Refer to pages: 15, 56

0	½	1	2	3	4	5	6	7	8	9	10	50	100	500	1000
零	半	一	二	三	四	五	六	七	八	九	十	十五	百	百五	千
		壹	貳	叁	肆	伍	陸	柒	捌	玖	拾	拾伍	佰	佰伍	仟

KWANGTUNG, 2 Cents, Y-418

七 7

year

The Chinese 'yr' number on this coin translates to 7.
From the 'yr'/Date (AD) Conversion Table,
page 56, 'yr' 7 indicates 1918 (AD).

Beginning of
Republic   + 'yr' -1 = Date (AD)
1912   + 7 -1 = 1918 (AD)

Note: This is an example of a 'yr' number of
one Chinese character.

GENERAL ISSUE, Dollar, Y-336

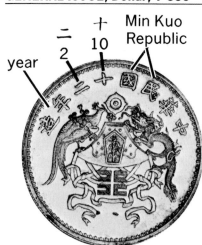

二 2
十 10
Min Kuo Republic
year

The Chinese 'yr' number on this coin translates to 10 and 2. To make this a useable number, do as follows:
     10 + 2 = 12
From the 'yr'/Date (AD) Conversion Table,
page 56, 'yr' 12 indicates 1923 (AD).

Beginning of
Republic   + 'yr' -1 = Date (AD)
1912   + 12 -1 = 1923 (AD)

Note: This is an example of a 'yr' number of
two Chinese characters.
Note: Read Chinese R to L.

Refer to pages: 15, 56

0	½	1	2	3	4	5	6	7	8	9	10	50	100	500	1000
零	半	一	二	三	四	五	六	七	八	九	十	十五	百	百五	千
		壹	貳	叄	肆	伍	陸	柒	捌	玖	拾	拾伍	佰	佰伍	仟

KANSU, Dollar, Y-410

The Chinese 'yr' number on this coin translates to 10 and 7. To make this a useable number, do as follows:

10 + 7 = 17

From the 'yr'/Date (AD) Conversion Table,
page 56, 'yr' 17 indicates 1928 (AD).

Beginning of
Republic   + 'yr' -1 = Date (AD)
1912   + 17 -1 = 1928 (AD)

Note: This is an example of a 'yr' number with
two Chinese characters.
Note: Read Chinese R to L.

GENERAL ISSUE, Dollar, Y-344

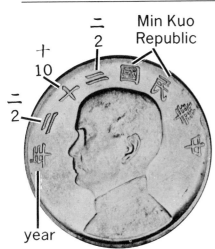

The Chinese 'yr' number on this coin translates to 2, 10 and 1. To make this a useable
number, do as follows:

(2 x 10) + 2 = 22

From the 'yr'/Date (AD) Conversion Table,
page 56, 'yr' 22 indicates 1933 (AD).

Beginning of
Republic   + 'yr' -1 = Date (AD)
1912   + 22 -1 = 1933 (AD)

Note: This is an example of a 'yr' number of
three Chinese characters.
Note: Read Chinese from R to L.

CHINA/Republic (Mainland)
(YrRep) YEAR OF REPUBLIC
CHINESE

Refer to pages: 15, 56

0	½	1	2	3	4	5	6	7	8	9	10	50	100	500	1000
零	半	一	二	三	四	五	六	七	八	九	十	十五	百	百五	千
		壹	貳	叁	肆	伍	陸	柒	捌	玖	拾	拾伍	佰	佰伍	仟

GENERAL ISSUE, 20 Cash, Y-325a

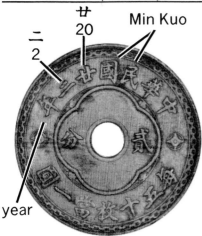

二
2

廿
20

Min Kuo

year

The Chinese 'yr' number on this coin translates to 20 and 2. To make this a useable number, do as follows:

20 + 2 = 22

From the 'yr'/Date (AD) Conversion Table, page 56, 'yr' 22 indicates 1933 (AD).

Beginning of
Republic   + 'yr' -1 = Date (AD)
1912   + 22 -1 = 1933 (AD)

Note: This is an example of a 'yr' number of two Chinese characters.
Note: Read Chinese from R to L.
Note: This is a good example of the use of 20
, instead of the more commonly used
(2 x 10) + 2 = 22.

DATES ON COINS OF CHINA — Republic
Conversion Table
'yr' number/Chinese 'yr' number/Date (AD)

Yr	Chinese Year	(AD)	Yr	Chinese Year	(AD)	Yr	Chinese Year	(AD)
1	一	1912	11	一十	1922	21	一十二	1932
2	二	1913	12	二十	1923	22	二十二	1933
3	三	1914	13	三十	1924	23	三十二	1934
4	四	1915	14	四十	1925	24	四十二	1935
5	五	1916	15	五十	1926	25	五十二	1936
6	六	1917	16	六十	1927	26	六十二	1937
7	七	1918	17	七十	1928	27	七十二	1938
8	八	1919	18	八十	1929	28	八十二	1939
9	九	1920	19	九十	1930	29	九十二	1940
10	十	1921	20	十二	1931	30	十三	1941

Conversion Table
'yr' number/Chinese 'yr' number/Date (AD)

Yr	Chinese Year	(AD)	Yr	Chinese Year	(AD)	Yr	Chinese Year	(AD)
31	一十三	1942	50	十五	1961	70	十七	1981
32	二十三	1943	51	一十五	1962	71	一十七	1982
33	三十三	1944	52	二十五	1963	72	二十七	1983
34	四十三	1945	53	三十五	1964	73	三十七	1984
35	五十三	1946	54	四十五	1965	74	四十七	1985
36	六十三	1947	55	五十五	1966	75	五十七	1986
37	七十三	1948	56	六十五	1967	76	六十七	1987
38	八十三	1949	57	七十五	1968	77	七十七	1988
	(Taiwan)		58	八十五	1969	78	八十七	1989
39	九十三	1950	59	九十五	1970	79	九十七	1990
40	十四	1951	60	十六	1971	80	十八	1991
41	一十四	1952	61	一十六	1972	81	一十八	1992
42	二十四	1953	62	二十六	1973	82	二十八	1993
43	三十四	1954	63	三十六	1974	83	三十八	1994
44	四十四	1955	64	四十六	1975	84	四十八	1995
45	五十四	1956	65	五十六	1976	85	五十八	1996
46	六十四	1957	66	六十六	1977	86	六十八	1997
47	七十四	1958	67	七十六	1978	87	七十八	1998
48	八十四	1959	68	八十六	1979	88	八十八	1999
49	九十四	1960	69	九十六	1980	89	九十八	2000

Note: Always read Chinese right to left.
CHINA/Republic (Mainland) 1912-1949 AD
CHINA/Republic (Taiwan) 1950- AD
Mathematics: 1912 (YrRep) + 'year' on coin -1 = (AD) date

Refer to pages: 15

0	½	1	2	3	4	5	6	7	8	9	10	50	100	500	1000
零	半	一	二	三	四	五	六	七	八	九	十	十五	百	百五	千
		壹	貳	叁	肆	伍	陸	柒	捌	玖	拾	拾伍	佰	佰伍	仟

REPUBLIC SECTION, Dollar, Y-332

"Empire of China"

"Beginning of Hung Hsien (period)"

This coin has no visible date but it is listed in the SCWC as 1916 (AD).
If you are confused with a (YR) dated coin that was issued almost four years after the Republic was established, you have a right to be. Now, Hung Hsein (Yuan Shih K'ai) set himself up as Emperor in December of 1915 (AD) and died soon afterwards in the summer of 1916 (AD). For purposes of coin dating, we will use 1915 (AD).

HUNAN, 10 Cash, Y-401

"The First Year of Hung Huan (Hsein)".

This coin has no visible date but it is listed in the SCWC as 1915 (AD).
For purposes of coin dating, we will assume the correct Accession Date for Hung Hsein as being 1915 (AD).

DATES ON COINS OF CHINA/Manchukuo/Japanese Puppet

The Dating System used is as follows:

(YR) Year of Reign — There were two rulers of Manchukuo, Ta Tung (1932-1934 AD) and Kang Teh (1934-1945 AD).

Calculations for (YR) Dating
Accession year + 'yr' -1 = Date (AD)

Note: In 1932, Japan set up the Puppet State of Manchukuo in the northeastern provinces of China. The first ruler was Ta Tung (1932-1934 AD). In 1934, this was converted to an Empire status with Hsuan Tung, the ousted Emperor of China as, the titular head. This new ruler, under the name of Kang Teh (1934-1945 AD) fronted for the Japanese and the territory rapidly grew as the Japanese armies invaded more of China. This continued until the end of World War II when the Russians took control of what had been the original Manchukuo and in 1946 they turned control over to the new People's Republic of China.

Refer to pages: 7-15, 60

0	½	1	2	3	4	5	6	7	8	9	10	50	100	500	1000
零	半	一	二	三	四	五	六	七	八	九	十	十五	百	百五	千
		壹	貳	叁	肆	伍	陸	柒	捌	玖	拾	拾伍	佰	佰伍	仟

MANCHUKUO, Fen, Y-2

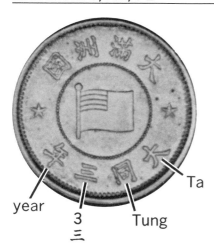

year 3 三 Tung Ta

The 'yr' number on this coin translates to 2.

Accession year + 'yr' -1 = Date (AD)

1932 + 2 -1 = 1933 (AD)

Ta Tung was the first ruler of Manchukuo (1932-1934 AD). His Accession date is 1932 (AD).

CHINA/Manchukuo/Japanese Puppet
(YR) YEAR OF REIGN
CHINESE

Refer to pages: 7-15, 60

0	½	1	2	3	4	5	6	7	8	9	10	50	100	500	1000
零	半	一	二	三	四	五	六	七	八	九	十	十五	百	百五	千
		壹	貳	叁	肆	伍	陸	柒	捌	玖	拾	拾伍	佰	佰伍	仟

MANCHUKUO, 5 Fen, Y-11

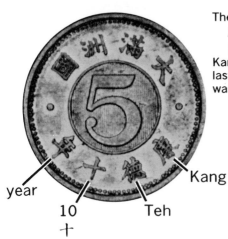

year
10
十
Kang
Teh

The 'yr' number on this coin translates to 10.

Accession year + 'yr' -1 = Date (AD)

1934   + 10 -1 = 1943 (AD)

Kang Teh (1934-1945 AD) was the second and last ruler of Manchukuo. His Accession date was 1934 (AD).

DATES ON COINS OF CHINA/Manchukuo/Japanese Puppet

Conversion Table
'yr' number/Chinese 'yr' number/Date (AD)
TA TUNG REIGN (1932-1934 AD)

'yr'	Chinese Year	(AD)	'yr'	Chinese Year	(AD)	'yr'	Chinese Year	(AD)
1	一	1932	2	二	1933	3	三	1934

KANG TEH REIGN (1934-1945 AD)

'yr'	Chinese Year	(AD)	'yr'	Chinese Year	(AD)	'yr'	Chinese Year	(AD)
1	一	1934	5	五	1938	9	九	1942
2	二	1935	6	六	1939	10	十	1943
3	三	1936	7	七	1940	11	一十	1944
4	四	1937	8	八	1941	12	二十	1945

DATES ON COINS OF CHINA/Sinkiang

Although it isn't the intent of this book to treat each Province of China, or subdivisions of any country, individually, this huge Province of western China is probably worth special mention. Due to the diversity of races, languages, and religions, the Coin Dating Systems also come in many forms.

The Dating Systems used are as follows:

(AH) Mohammedan Era — Most of the dated coins of Sinkiang are according to this system. For more information on (AH) dating, refer to, "Dates on Coins of Arabic Influenced Countries".

(CD) Cyclical Dating — A few of the coins of Sinkiang are dated according to this system. For more information on (CD) dating, refer to, "Cyclical Dating on Chinese Coins".

(YR) Year of Reign — Some coins of Sinkiang are dated according to this system. For more information, refer to, "Dates on Coins of China/Empire".

(nd) No Date — Most coins of Sinkiang have no dates.

Note: There will be no specific examples of Sinkiang coins.

DATES ON COINS OF CHINA/TIBET

The Dating Systems used are as follows:

(YR) Year of Reign — On Tibetan coins, the (YR) Year of Reign Dates refer to the Reign of some certain Chinese Emperor. The 'yr' number on the coins may appear either in Chinese or Tibetan numerals.

Note: The 'yr' number found on the coin is the actual year during the Reign that the coin was minted.

(CD) Cyclical Dating — These Tibetan dates conform to a 60 year recurring pattern. The Tibetan system is similar to the Cyclical Dating System used in China, but it is not interchangeable. To illustrate this:

1980 (AD) = 16th cycle, plus 54 years (Tibetan) = 1014 (Tibetan)
1980 (AD) = 77th cycle, plus 57 years (Chinese) = 4677 (Chinese)

Calculations for (CD) Dating)

(cycle x 60 years) + 'yr' on coin = (cycle years)

As the Tibetan Cyclical Dating System had its beginning in 966 (AD), the 966 must be added to the (cycle years) to determine the proper (AD) date.

(cycle years) + 966 = Date (AD)

Note: The 'yr' number found on the coin is the actual year during the cycle that the coin was minted.

NUMERALS

1	༡ གཅིག	9	༩ དགུ	16	༡༦ བཅུ་དྲུག	22	༢༢ ཉེར་གཉིས
2	༢ གཉིས	10	༡༠ བཅུ	17	༡༧ བཅུ་བདུན	23	༢༣ ཉེར་གསུམ
3	༣ གསུམ		or བཅུ་ཐམ་པ	18	༡༨ བཅོ་བརྒྱད	24	༢༤ ཉེར་བཞི
4	༤ བཞི	11	༡༡ བཅུ་གཅིག	19	༡༩ བཅུ་དགུ	25	༢༥ ཉེར་ལྔ
5	༥ ལྔ	12	༡༢ བཅུ་གཉིས	20	༢༠ ཉི་ཤུ	26	༢༦ ཉེར་དྲུག
6	༦ དྲུག	13	༡༣ བཅུ་གསུམ	21	༢༡ ཉི་ཤུ་རྩ་གཅིག	27	༢༧ ཉེར་བདུན
7	༧ བདུན	14	༡༤ བཅུ་བཞི		or ཉེར་གཅིག	28	༢༨ ཉེར་བརྒྱད
8	༨ བརྒྱད	15	༡༥ བཅོ་ལྔ				

Refer to pages: 7-15

0	½	1	2	3	4	5	6	7	8	9	10	50	100	500	1000
o	7/2	7	2	3	C	U	b	2	ſ	P	7o	Uo	7oo	Uoo	7ooo
零	半	一	二	三	四	五	六	七	八	九	十	十五	百	百五	千

TIBET, Sho, C-67

The 'yr' number on this coin translates to 57.

Accession date + 'yr' -1 = Date (AD)

1736   + 57 -1 = 1792 (AD)

As the Chinese Emperor Ch'ien Lung (1736-1796 AD) had the only Reign that lasted for 57 years, it is obvious this coin was minted during his Reign. His Accession date is 1736 (AD).

5
U

7
2

TIBET, ½ Tangka, C-66

五
5

Nien
(Year)

10 十

8
八

Note: Read Chinese R to L.

The 'yr' number on this coin translates to (5 x 10) + 8 = 58

Accession date + 'yr' -1 = Date (AD)

1736   + 58 -1 = 1793 (AD)

As the Chinese Emperor Ch'ien Lung (1736-1796 AD) had the only reign that lasted for 58 years, it is obvious this coin was minted during his reign. His Accession date is 1736 (AD).

Refer to pages: 7-15,

0	½	1	2	3	4	5	6	7	8	9	10	50	100	500	1000
零	半	一	二	三	四	五	六	七	八	九	十	十五	百	百五	千
		١	١١	١١١	Ⅹ	Ꝑ	⊥	⊥	⊥	夂	十	Ꝑ十	١百	Ꝑ百	١千

TIBET, Sho, C-72.2

六
6
Ch'ien

Nien
(Year)

—10 十

Lung

Note: Read Chinese R to L.
The 'yr' number on this coin translates to (6 x 10) = 60

Accession date + 'yr' -1 = Date (AD)
1736 + 60 -1 = 1795 (AD)

As the Chinese Emperor Ch'ien Lung (1736-1796 AD) had the only reign that lasted for 60 years, it is obvious this coin was minted during his reign. His Accession date is 1736 (AD).

TIBET, Sho, C-93

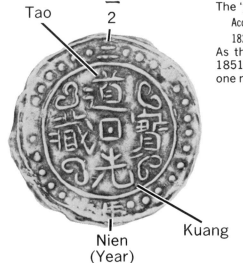

Tao
二
2

The 'yr' number on this coin translates to 2.

Accession date + 'yr' -1 = Date (AD)
1821 + 2 -1 = 1822 (AD)

As the Chinese Emperor Tao Kuang (1821-1851 AD) had a shorter reign than Ch'ien Lung one must identify his characters carefully.

Kuang

Nien
(Year)

CHINA/Tibet
(YR) YEAR OF REIGN
CHINESE

Refer to pages: 7-15, 18

0	½	1	2	3	4	5	6	7	8	9	10	50	100	500	1000
o	⁷⁄₂	𑲦	⁊	⁊	𑲤	𑲪	𑲬	𑲮	𑲰	𑲲	𑲦o	𑲪o	𑲮oo	𑲤oo	𑲮ooo

TIBET, 1 Srang, Y-12

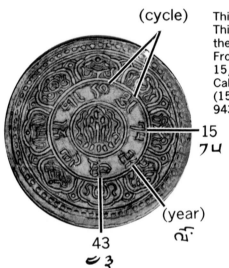

(cycle)

15
𑲮𑲪

(year)
འི་

43
𑲬𑲴

This coin has the Tibetan numbers 15 and 43. This is the (CD) which means it was struck in the 15th cycle and the 43rd 'yr' of that cycle. From the Tibetan Cyclical Date Chart, chart F.
15/43 = 1909 (AD)
Calculations:
(15 x 60) + 43 = 943 (cycle years)
943 (cycle years) + 966 (AD) = 1909 (AD)

TIBET, 10 Srang, Y-29a

འི་
(year)

2𑲰
24

བཅུ་དྲུག་
16

(cycle)
ꞮÖ·ྱཅ·

This coin has the Tibetan numbers 16 and 24. This is the (CD) which means it was struck in the 16th cycle and the 24th 'yr' of that cycle. From the Tibetan Cyclical Date Chart, chart F.
16/24 = 1950 (AD)
Calculations:
(16 x 60) + 24 = 984 (cycle years)
984 (cycle years) + 966 (AD) = 1950 (AD)

Refer to pages: 7-15, 18

0	½	1	2	3	4	5	6	7	8	9	10	50	100	500	1000
o	⁷⁄₂	ᱏ	᱒	ᱩ	ᡱ	ㄩ	ㄖ	ᱛ	ᱝ	ᱟ	ᱏo	ㄩo	ᱛoo	ㄩoo	ᱛooo

TIBET, 1 Tangka, Y-A13

7
1

ㄩ
5

2
᱒

4
ᡶ

This coin has the Tibetan numbers 15 and 24.
This is the (CD) which means it was struck in
the 15th cycle and the 24th 'yr' of that cycle.
From the Tibetan Cyclical Date Chart, chart F.
15/24 = 1890 (AD)
Calculations:
(15 x 60) + 24 = 924 (cycle years)
924 (cycle years) + 966 (AD) = 1890 (AD)

TIBET, 3 Srang, Y-26

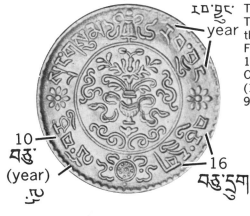

year

10
(year)

16

This coin has the Tibetan Numbers 16 and 10.
This is the (CD) which means it was struck in
the 16th cycle and the 10th 'yr' of that cycle.
From the Tibetan Cyclical Date Chart, chart F.
16/10 = 1936 (AD)
Calculations:
(16 x 60) + 10 = 970 (cycle years)
970 (cycle years) + 966 (AD) = 1936 (AD)

Refer to pages: 5, 21

0	½	1	2	3	4	5	6	7	8	9	10	50	100	500	1000
o	⁷⁄₂	7	2	₹	⊂	५	Ƀ	Ꝓ	ſ	℗	7o	५o	7oo	५oo	7ooo

TIBET, 5 Sho, Y-28

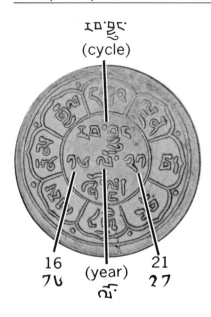

ꓘꓠ·ꞹꓫ·
(cycle)

16
7ꓑ
(year)
ꞩ·
21
2 7

This coin has the Tibetan numbers 16 and 21. This is the (CD) which means it was struck in the 16th cycle and the 21st 'yr' of that cycle. From the Tibetan Cyclical Date Chart, chart G.
16/21 = 1947 (AD)
Calculations:
(16 x 60) + 21 = 981 (cycle years)
981 (cycle years) + 966 (AD) = 1947 (AD)

DATES ON COINS OF CHINA/Soviets

The Dating Systems used are as follows:

(AD) Christian Era — Some coins of the China/Soviets were poorly made and had (AD) dates where 4's were turned backwards, and 3's which looked like 8's. There will be no examples of these (AD) dated coins.

(dt) Direct Translation — Some coins of the China/Soviets had dates in Chinese characters which translated directly to proper (AD) date. Coin Example No. 2 is unusual as it shows a case where Chinese is read from L to R, instead of the usual R to L.

Note: After Chiang Kai-shek killed a great number of his former comrades (the purges of the mid-1920's) the remaining Chinese Communists moved south of the Yangtze and set up business in the Provinces of Fukien, Kiangsi, Hupeh and Honan. Here they established Communes, or Provincial political groups called "Soviets". Although they had plenty of Russian advisors, there was no direct control by the U.S.S.R.

Refer to page: 15

0	½	1	2	3	4	5	6	7	8	9	10	50	100	500	1000
零	半	一	二	三	四	五	六	七	八	九	十	十五	百	百五	千
		壹	貳	叁	肆	伍	陸	柒	捌	玖	拾	拾伍	佰	佰伍	仟

CHINA/Szechuan-Shensi Soviet District, 500 Cash, Y-512.1

The date number on this coin translates to 1934.
Note: Read Chinese from R to L.

    Date (dt)   = Date (AD)
    1934 (dt)   = 1934 (AD)

year   4   3   9   1
       四   三   九   一

CHINA/Hupeh-Honan-Anhwei Soviet District, Dollar, Y-503

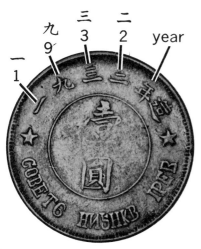

九   三   二
9   3   2   year
一
1

The date number on this coin translates to 1932.
Note: This example is an unusual specimen where the Chinese characters are read from L to R, instead of R to L. It is not known why this was done but it might have been the result of the many Russian advisors who were very busy helping the Chinese Communists at that time.

    Date (dt)   = Date (AD)
    1932 (dt)   = 1932 (AD)

DATE ON COINS OF CHINA/Republic (Taiwan)

The Dating System used is as follows:

(YrRep) Year of Republic — This Dating System had its beginning in 1912 and, even though the Chinese Communists caused the Republic Government to flee to Taiwan in 1949, they have continued to use the same Coin Dating System used on the Mainland.

Calculations for (YrRep) Dating

Beginning year of Republic   + 'yr' -1 = Date (AD)
1912   + 'yr' -1 = Date (AD)

Refer to pages: 15, 18, 56

0	½	1	2	3	4	5	6	7	8	9	10	50	100	500	1000
零	半	一	二	三	四	五	六	七	八	九	十	十五	百	百五	千
		壹	貳	叁	肆	伍	陸	柒	捌	玖	拾	拾伍	佰	佰伍	仟

CHINA (Taiwan), 20 Cents, Y-534

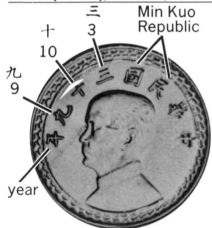

十 10
三 3
Min Kuo Republic
九 9
year

The Chinese 'yr' number on this coin translates to 3, 10 and 9. To make this a useable number, do as follows:

(3 x 10) + 9 = 'yr'
30 + 9 = 39

Beginning of
Republic   + 'yr' -1 = Date (AD)
1912   + 39 -1 = 1950 (AD)

Note: Read Chinese from R to L.
The (YrRep) Dating on China (Taiwan) coins is just a continuation of (YrRep) China (Mainland). From the 'yr'/Chinese 'yr'/Date (AD) Conversion Table on page 56, 'yr' 39 = 1950 (AD).

CHINA (Taiwan), 5 Dollars, Y-548

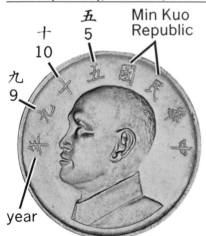

十 10
五 5
Min Kuo Republic
九 9
year

The Chinese 'yr' number on this coin translates to 6, 10 and 3. To make this a useable number, do as follows:

(5 x 10) + 9 = 'yr'
50 + 9 = 59

Beginning of
Republic   + 'yr' -1 = Date (AD)
1912   + 59 -1 = 1970 (AD)

Note: Read Chinese from R to L.
The (YrRep) Dating on China (Taiwan) coins is just a continuation of (YrRep) China (Mainland). From the 'yr'/Chinese 'yr'/Date (AD) Conversion Table on page 56, 'yr' 59 = 1970 (AD).

DATES ON COINS OF ETHIOPIA

The Dating System used is as follows:

(EE) Ethiopian Era — This Dating System had its beginning 7 years and 8 months after the advent of (AD) dating.

Calculations for (EE) Dating

Date (EE) + 8 = Date (AD)

Note: As the (EE) Dating System began 7 years and 8 months after the (AD) system, it is possible to have two different (EE) dates on coins for the same (AD) year.

Refer to page: 10

0	½	1	2	3	4	5	6	7	8	9	10	50	100	500	1000
◆		δ̄	Ḇ	Γ̄	Ō	Ċ̄	ӡ̄	Ż	Ṯ	Ṵ	ī	Ÿ	Q̣	Ċ̄ Q̣	ī Q̣
			20 Ҳ̄	30 ₥̄	40 Ӱ̄		60 Ṯ̄	70 Ḟ̄	80 Ṳ̄	90 ₮̄					

ETHIOPIA, 1/100 Bir, Y-1

10   8   100   80   9
ī   Ṯ̄   Q̣   Ṳ̄   Ṵ

The date number on this coin, in Ethiopian numerals, translates to 10, 8, 100, 80, and 9. Now, to make this into a useable number, do as follows:

(10 + 8) x 100	+ 80 + 9 =	(EE)
(18 x 100)	+ 80 + 9 =	(EE)
1800	+ 80 + 9 =	1889 (EE)
Date (EE)	+ 8 =	Date (AD)
1889	+ 8 =	1897 (AD)

ETHIOPIA, 1 Cent, Y-30

10   9   100   30   6
ī   Ṵ   Q̣   ₥̄   ӡ̄

The date number on this coin, in Ethiopian numerals, translates to 10, 9, 100, 30 and 6. Now, to make this into a useable number, do as follows:

(10 + 9) x 100	+ 30 + 6 =	(EE)
(19 x 100)	+ 30 + 6 =	(EE)
1900	+ 30 + 6 =	1936 (EE)
Date (EE)	+ 8 =	Date (AD)
1936	+ 8 =	1944 (AD)

DATES ON COINS OF INDIA

The dates on coins of the Indian Princely States and Independent Kingdoms are made up of many Numeral Systems, and combinations of Numeral Systems. The most common are shown below.

STANDARD INTERNATIONAL NUMERAL SYSTEMS

	0	½	1	2	3	4	5	6	7	8	9	10	50	100	500	1000
WESTERN	0	½	1	2	3	4	5	6	7	8	9	10	50	100	500	1000
ARABIC-TURKISH	•	١/٢	١	٢	٣	٤	٥	٦	٧	٨	٩	١٠	٥٠	١٠٠	٥٠٠	١٠٠٠
MALAY-PERSIAN	•	١/٢	١	٢	٣	٤	٥	٦	٧	٨	٩	١٠	٥٠	١٠٠	٥٠٠	١٠٠٠
EASTERN ARABIC	۰	١/٢	١	٢	٣	٤	٥	٦	٧	٨	٩	١۰	۵۱۰	١۰۰	۵۱۰۰	١۰۰۰
HYDERABAD ARABIC	۰	١/٢	١	٢	٣	٤	٥	٦	٧	٨	٩	١۰	۵۰١۰	۵۰۱۰۰	۵۰۰	۵۰۰ ١۰۰۰
INDIAN (Sanskrit)	०	३/२	९	२	३	४	५	६	७	८	९	९०	४०	९००	४००	९०००
ASSAMESE	০	৬/২	৭	২	৩	৪	৫	৬	৭	৮	২	৭০	৫০	৭০০	৫০০	৭০০০
BEGALI	০	৩/২	২	২	৩	৪	৫	৩	৭	৮	৩	২০	৮০	২০০	৮০০	২০০০
GUJARATI	૦	૯/૨	૧	૨	૩	૪	૫	૬	૭	૮	૯	૧૦	૪૦	૧૦૦	૪૦૦	૧૦૦૦
KUTCH	૦	૧/૨	૧	૨	૩	૪	૫	૬ or ૬	૭	૮	૯	૧૦	૪૦	૧૦૦	૪૦૦	૧૦૦૦
NAVANAGAR	૦	૯/૨	૯	૨	૩	૪	૫	૬	૭	૮	૯	૯૦	૪૦	૯૦૦	૪૦૦	૯૦૦૦

INDIA
General

For centuries, the Rajahs and Princes governed the Indian Princely States and it seems, in order to prove they were worthy rulers, they rushed out and had coins minted — many of poor quality. To complicate the fact, India has fourteen major languages and hundreds of minor languages and dialects. This great number of languages, along with widespread illiteracy, has greatly hindered social and economic development.

When India gained its independence from Great Britain, in 1950, its language problems seemed to increase. The new Constitution declared that English would remain the official Government language for a period of fifteen years and, sure enough, in 1965 English became an "associate" language and Hindi took its place. As only one half of the population spoke Hindi, the remainder decried that only the Hindi speaking segment would be eligible for Civil Service jobs and the better positions in private enterprise.

The hundreds of Indian Princely States were generally composed of people who spoke a common language but when the new government of the Republic disbanded the Princely States, trouble began. In 1956, they began reducing the number of Federal States from 27 to 14. This act threw people of different languages into the same political subdivision, which was usually dominated by the majority who spoke the same language. Great dissatisfaction occurred and the Government was forced to drive some of the newly formed States — such as Bombay into two new States, Gujarat and Maharashtra.

The main northern languages are the Indo-European group which includes: Assamese, Bengali, Gujarati, Hindi, Kashmiri, Marathi, Oriys, Punjabi and Rajasthani, all from the Sanskrit basis. The Dravidian languages of the south are Kannada, Malayalam, Tamil and Telugu. Most of the tribal people, in both areas, speak their own language or dialect. As you can see from this, we are fortunate when dating coins of India that there are fewer Numeral and Dating Systems, than languages.

DATES ON COINS OF INDIA/Mughal Empire

The Dating System used is as follows:

(IL) Ilahi Era — This Dating System was used on coin of the Mughal Empire about 1584-1605 (AD). The mathematics to change an (IL) date to an (AD) date are as follows:

Calculations for (IL) Dating
Date (IL) 1554 Date (AD)

TABLE
(IL) Dates To (AD) Dates

(IL)	(AD)	(IL)	(AD)	(IL)	(AD)
30	1584	37	1591	44	1598
31	1585	38	1592	45	1599
32	1586	39	1593	46	1600
33	1587	40	1594	47	1601
34	1588	41	1595	48	1602
35	1589	42	1596	49	1603
36	1590	43	1597	50	1604
				51	1605

Note: It is possible to have a one year error.

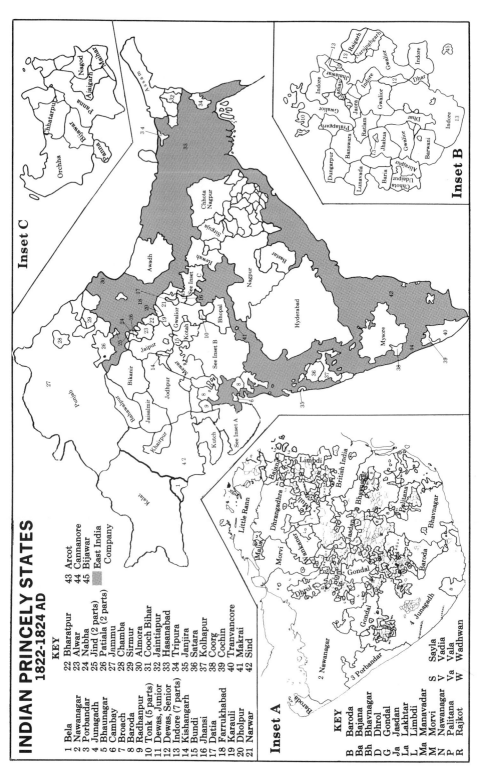

INDIAN PRINCELY STATES
1822-1824 AD

KEY

1	Bela	22	Bharatpur
2	Nawanagar	23	Alwar
3	Porbandar	24	Nabha
4	Junagadh	25	Jind (2 parts)
5	Bhaunagar	26	Patiala (2 parts)
6	Cambay	27	Jammu
7	Broach	28	Chamba
8	Baroda	29	Sirmur
9	Radhanpur	30	Almora
10	Tonk (5 parts)	31	Cooch Bihar
11	Dewas, Junior	32	Jaintiapur
12	Dewas, Senior	33	Hasanabad
13	Indore (7 parts)	34	Tripura
14	Kishangarh	35	Janjira
15	Bundi	36	Satara
16	Jhansi	37	Kolhapur
17	Datia	38	Coorg
18	Farrukhabad	39	Cochin
19	Karauli	40	Tranvancore
20	Dholpur	41	Makrai
21	Narwar	42	Sind
		43	Arcot
		44	Cannanore
		45	Bijawar

■ East India Company

Inset C

Inset B

Inset A

KEY

B	Baroda
Ba	Bajana
Bh	Bhavnagar
D	Dhrol
G	Gondal
Ja	Jasdan
La	Lakhtar
L	Limbdi
Ma	Manavadar
M	Morvi
N	Nawanagar
P	Palitana
R	Rajkot
S	Sayla
V	Vadia
Va	Vala
W	Wadhwan

DATES ON COINS OF INDIA/Indore

The Dating System used is as follows:

(FE) Fasli Era — This is a Solar Year dating system and is similar to the (FE) dates on coins of the Maratha Confederacy except for spread between the (FE) date and the (AD) date. With the Maratha (FE) system, the spread is 590 years, but with the Indore system, the spread is from 592 to 595 years. Due to this, we will assume a spread of 593 years so we can establish a formula. With this assumption, the mathematics to change an Indore (FE) date to an (AD) date are as follows:

Calculations for Indore (FE) Dating

Date Indore (FE) + 593 = Date (AD)

Note: There is the possibility that the true date could be plus or minus two years.

DATES ON COINS OF INDIA/Travancore

The Dating System used is as follows:

(ME) Malabar Era — This is a small Dating System used in the Indian Princely State of Travancore. It had its beginning about 824-825 (AD). The mathematics to change a (ME) date to an (AD) date are as follows:

Calculations for (ME) Dating

Date (ME) + 824 = Date (AD)

Note: There is the possibility of a one year error when dating (ME) coins.

DATES ON COINS OF INDIA/Maratha Confederacy

The Dating System used is as follows:

(FE) Fasli Era — This is a Solar Year dating system and had its beginning with the Conversion of Muhammad in 591 (AD). To change a (FE) date to an (AD) date, the mathematics are as follows:

Calculations for (FE) Dating

Date (FE) + 590 = Date (AD)

(dt) Direct Translation — These dates are shown in some type of numerals, other than western, but they translate directly to the correct (AD) date.

Note: The great number of Dating examples used for the Indian Princely States may seem excessive, but it was done to show the different Numerals Systems, also.

INDIA/Mughal Empire
(IL) ILAHI ERA
ARABIC (Persian)

Refer to pages: 5, 10

0	½	1	2	3	4	5	6	7	8	9	10	50	100	500	1000
·	۱/۲	۱	۲	۳	٤	٥	٦	۷	۸	۹	۱۰	۵۰	۱۰۰	۵۰۰	۱۰۰۰

MUGHAL EMPIRE, ½ Rupee, KM-63.1

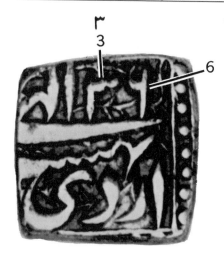

۳
3

6

The date number on this coin translates to 36.

Date (IL)	+ 1553 = Date (AD)
36	+ 1553 = 1589 (AD)

DATES ON COINS OF INDIA/Princely States

The Dating Systems used are as follows:

(AH) Mohammedan Era —The (AH) Dating System is most often used and they will surely provide a challenge. With such a wide variety of poorly made coins, the dates will be hard to find and they may be in any, or a combination of, the various Arabic numeral systems. Refer to, "Dates on Coins of Arabic Influenced Countries".

(VS) Vikrama Samvat Era — This Dating System is widely used, especially amongst the Indian Princely States. The (VS) system had its beginning on October 18, 58 (BC).
Calculations for (VS) Dating
Date (VS) -57 = Date (AD)

(SE) Saka Era — This Dating System is found almost exclusively in the Indian Princely States and had its beginning on March 3, 78 (AD).
Calculations for (SE) Dating
Date (SE) + 78 = Date (AD)

DATES ON COINS OF INDIA/Cooch Behar

The Dating System used is as follows:

(CB) Cooch Behar Era — This dating system was introduced in the Independent Kingdom of Cooch Behar during the Mughal Empire. It had its beginning in 1510 (AD) and the mathematics to change a (CB) date to an (AD) date are as follows:

Calculations for (CB) Dating
Date (CB) + 1510 = Date (AD)

DATES ON COINS OF INDIA/Mysore

The Dating System used is as follows:

(AM) Maludi Era — This Dating System was used in the Indian Independent Kingdom of Mysore from 1215-1227 (AM)/1786-1795 (AD). This Dating System had its beginning in 1786 (AD) and the mathematics to change an (AM) date to an (AD) date are as follows:

Calculations for (AM) Dating
Date (AM) + 571 = Date (AD)

Note No. 1: — The last four years of this dating system (1224-1227 AM) often have Arabic letters that also indicate the mint year of the coin. The examples are shown below:

Alif	1 or		AM1224
Be	or		AM1225
Te	or		AM1226
Se	or		AM1227

Dating

Sultan Tipu used Hijri years on his coins from AH1197 to AH1201. Thereafter he instituted the Mauludi era (AM), which used solar years, 14 years advanced from the Hijri years. They are indicated on the coins by being written in Arabic numerals from right to left, the opposite of normal usage. The Mauludi years were from 1215 to his death in 1227. The last four of these were often indicated by letters rather than numbers. thus Arabic ALIF = Mauludi 1224, BE = 1225, TE = 1226, SE = 1227. Many blundered dates exist on the copper coins. Two digit regnal years were also written from right to left.

Note No. 2 — Many coins of the (AM) Dating System have Regnal years ('yr' numbers) displayed but these are of no consequence when dating the coins. The date of the coin is the (AM) date displayed and can be converted to the correct (AD) mint year by use of the formula above.

Note No. 3 — The (AM) date numbers on these coins are displayed in Arabic numerals. These numbers, however, are most often read from R to L, instead of the normal L to R.

Note No. 4 — With this dating system there is the possibility of being off by one year. For more accurate information, see the preamble to the Mysore/INDEPENDENT KINGDOM in your copy of "The Standard Guide to South Asian Coins and Paper Money".

INDIA/Princely States
(VS) VIKRAMA SAMVAT ERA
SANSKRIT

Refer to pages: 5, 10

0	½	1	2	3	4	5	6	7	8	9	10	50	100	500	1000
०	॥	१	२	३	४	५	६	७	८	९	१०	५०	१००	५००	१०००

BARODA, Rupee, Y-36a

The Sanskrit date number on this coin translates to 1953.

Date (VS)   -57 = Date (AD)

1953 (VS)   -57 = 1896 (AD)

BARODA, 2 Paisa, Y-32.2

The Sanskrit date number on this coin translates to 1947.

Date (VS)   -57 = Date (AD)

1947 (VS)   -57 = 1890 (AD)

Refer to pages: 1-5, 23-28

0	½	1	2	3	4	5	6	7	8	9	10	50	100	500	1000
0	૦½	૧	૨	૩	૪	૫	૬	૭	૮	૯	૧૦	૫૦	૧૦૦	૫૦૦	૧૦૦૦

CHAMBRA, Dokdo, Y-6.3

The Gujarati date number on this coin translates to 1948.

Date (VS)   -57 = Date (AD)
1964 (VS)   -57 = 1907 (AD)

Refer to pages: 5, 10

0	½	1	2	3	4	5	6	7	8	9	10	50	100	500	1000
•	۱/۲	۱	۲	۳	۴	۵	۶ or	۷	۸	۹	۱۰	۵۰	۱۰۰	۵۰۰	۱۰۰۰

INDORE, Rupee, Y-14.3

The date number on this coin translates to 1296.

Date Indore (FE) + 593 = Date (AD)
1296   + 593 = 1889 (AD)
Note: There is the possibility of a plus or minus error of two years.

Refer to pages: 1-5, 23-28

0	½	1	2	3	4	5	6	7	8	9	10	50	100	500	1000
0	૦૨	૧	૨	૩	૪	૫	૬	૭	૮	૯	૧૦	૫૦	૧૦૦	૫૦૦	૧૦૦૦

JAIPUR, Anna, Y-18

The Gujarati date number on this coin translates to 1943 (AD).

Date (dt)	= Date (AD)
1943 (dt)	= 1943 (AD)

JUNAGADH, Dokdo, Y-1

The Gujarati date number on this coin translates to 1935.

Date (VS)	-57	= Date (AD)
1935 (VS)	-57	= 1878 (AD)

Refer to pages: 5, 10

0	½	1	2	3	4	5	6	7	8	9	10	50	100	500	1000
0	১⁄₂	૧	૨	૩	૪	૫	૬	૭	૮	૯	૧૦	૫૦	૧૦૦	૫૦૦	૧૦૦૦

The coinage of Kutch is unusual as most coins bear two dates, one is VS while the other is AD. As the two years differ combinations may be encountered having 2 different VS dates for a particular AD date.

KUTCH, 1½ Dokda, Y-32.2

(VS)

The Kutch date number on this coin translates to 1944.

Date (VS)	-57	= Date (AD)
1944 (VS)	-57	= 1887 (AD)

1 9 4 4
૧ ૯ ૪ ૪

1 8 8 7

(AD)

INDIA/Princely States
(VS) VIKRAMA SAMVAT
KUTCH

Refer to pages: 5, 10

0	½	1	2	3	4	5	6	7	8	9	10	50	100	500	1000
0	१/२	१	२	३	४	५	६	७	८	९	१०	४०	१००	४००	१०००

KUTCH, 5 Kori, Y-37.3

(VS)

1 9 3 7
१ ९ ३ ७

The Kutch date number on this coin translates to 1937.

Date (VS)   -57 = Date (AD)
1937 (VS   -57 = 1880 (AD)

(AD)

1 8 8 1
१ ८ ८ १

Note: 1 year error is possible.

80

INDIA/Princely States
(VS) VIKRAMA SAMVAT
NAVANGAR

Refer to pages: 5, 10

0	½	1	2	3	4	5	6	7	8	9	10	50	100	500	1000
0	૧/૨	૧	૨	૩	૪	૫	૬ or ૬	૭	८	૮ᶜ or ૮	૧૦	૫૦	૧૦૦	૪૦૦	૧૦૦૦

NAWANAGER, 5 Kori, Y-16

The Navangar date number on this coin translates to 1947.

Date (VS)	-57 = Date (AD)
1947 (VS)	-57 = 1890 (AD)

NAWANAGER, Kori, Y-12

The Navangar date number on this coin translates to 1935.

Date (VS)	-57 = Date (AD)
1935 (VS)	-57-57 = 1878 (AD)

Refer to pages: 5, 10

0	½	1	2	3	4	5	6	7	8	9	10	50	100	500	1000

TRAVANCORE, ½ Rupee, Y-36.2

1086

Date (ME)   + 824 = Date (AD)
1086   + 824 = 1910 (AD)
Note: There is the possibility of a one year error.

TRAVANCORE, ½ Rupee, Y-47

1112

Date (ME)   + 824 = Date (AD)
1112   + 824 = 1936 (AD)
Note: There is a possibility of a one year error.

Refer to pages: 5, 10

0	½	1	2	3	4	5	6	7	8	9	10	50	100	500	1000
0	૧/૨	૧	૨	૩	૪	૫	૬	૭	૮	૯	૧૦	૫૦	૧૦૦	૫૦૦	૧૦૦૦

MARATHA CONFEDERACY, Rupee, KM-126

The date number on this coin translates to 1244.

Date (FE)	+ 590 = Date (AD)
1244	+ 590 = 1834 (AD)

MARATHA CONFEDERACY, Rupee, KM-122

The date number on this coin translates to (1)234.

Date (FE)	+ 590 = Date (AD)
1234	+ 590 = 1824 (AD)

INDIA/Independent Kingdoms
(SE) SAKA ERA
ASSAMESE

Refer to pages: 5, 10

0	½	1	2	3	4	5	6	7	8	9	10	50	100	500	1000
0	d/2	d	2	ꭎ	8	5	5	੧	४	2	d0	50	d00	500	d000

ASSAM, ¼ Rupee, KM-198

d ੧ 0 ੧
1 7 0 7

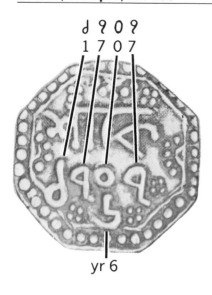

yr 6

The Assamese date number on this coin translates to 1707.

Date (SE)	+ 78 = Date (AD)
1707 (SE)	+ 78 = 1785 (AD)

ASSAM, Rupee, KM-215

5
5
0
0
1 7
d ੧

The Assamese date number on this coin translates to 1705.

Date (SE)	+ 78 = Date (AD)
1705 (SE)	+ 78 = 1783 (AD)

84

Refer to pages: 5, 10

0	½	1	2	3	4	5	6	7	8	9	10	50	100	500	1000
0	d/2	d	2	J	8	5	9	9	৮	৯	d0	50	d00	500	d000

COOCH BEHAR, Mohur, Y-6

The date number on this coin translates to 402.

Date (CB)	+ 1510 = Date (AD)
402	+ 1510 = 1912 (AD)

COOCH BEHAR, ½ Rupee, Y-9

The date number on this coin translates to 413.

Date (CB)	+ 1510 = Date (AD)
413	+ 1510 = 1923 (AD)

INDIA/Independent Kingdoms
(AM) MALUDI ERA
ARABIC

Refer to pages: 5, 10

0	½	1	2	3	4	5	6	7	8	9	10	50	100	500	1000
٥	١⁄٢	١	٢	٣	٣	٥	٤	٧	٨	٩	١٥	٥٥	١٥٥	٥٥٥	١٥٥٥

MYSORE, Paisa, KM-103.9
Letter Dates Type 2

Se

The date number on this coin translates to 1227.

Date (AM)	+ 571 = Date (AD)
1227	+ 571 = 1798 (AD)

Note: This coin displays "Se" which is the Arabic letter that indicates the (AM) year of the coin to be 1227.

MYSORE, Paisa, KM-103.12
Letter Dates Type 2

Alif (1)

4
2
2
1

The date number on this coin translates to 1224.

Date (AM)	+ 571 = Date (AD)
1224	+ 571 = 1795 (AD)

Note: This coin displays "1" (Alif) which is the Arabic letter that indicates the (AM) year of the coin to be 1224.

Refer to pages: 5, 10

0	½	1	2	3	4	5	6	7	8	9	10	50	100	500	1000
0	½ᵣ	١	٢	٣	٣ٔ	٥	٤	<	٨	٩	١٠	٥٠	١٠٠	٥٠٠	١٠٠٠

MYSORE, Paisa, KM-103.3

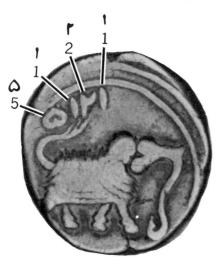

The date number on this coin translates to 1215.

Date (AM)   + 571 = Date (AD)
1215   + 571 = 1786 (AD)

Note: Read the Arabic date number from R to L.

MYSORE, Paisa, KM-53

The date number on this coin translates to 1218.

Date (AM)   + 571 = Date (AD)
1218   + 571 = 1789 (AD)

Note: Read the Arabic date number from R to L.

INDIA/Independent Kingdoms
(AM) MALUDI ERA
ARABIC

Refer to pages: 5, 10

0	½	1	2	3	4	5	6	7	8	9	10	50	100	500	1000
0	½ᵣ	١	٢	٣	٣	۵	۴	<	٨	٩	١٠	۵٠	١٠٠	۵٠٠	١٠٠٠

MYSORE, 2 Paisa, KM-104.2
Letter Dates Type 1

Alif

The date number on this coin translates to 1224.

Date (AM)   + 571 = Date (AD)
1224   + 571 = 1795 (AD)

Note: This coin displays "Alif" which is the Arabic letter that indicates the (AM) year of the coin to be 1224.

1
١

2
٢

2
٢

4
٣

Refer to pages: 5, 10

0	½	1	2	3	4	5	6	7	8	9	10	50	100	500	1000
o	١/r	١	r	٣	٣	٥	٤	<	٨	٩	١٥	٥٥	٥٥	٥٥٥	١٥٥٥

MYSORE, 2 Paisa, KM-104.4

Letter Dates Type 1

The date number on this coin translates to 1226.

Date (AM)	+ 571 = Date (AD)
1226	+ 571 = 1797 (AD)

Note: This coin displays "Te" which is the Arabic letter that indicates the (AM) year of the coin to be 1226.

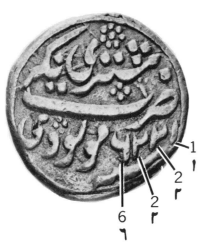

INDIA/Independent Kingdoms
(AM) MALUDI ERA
ARABIC

Refer to pages: 5, 10

0	½	1	2	3	4	5	6	7	8	9	10	50	100	500	1000
0	۱/ᵣ	۱	۲	۳	۴	۵	۶	۷	۸	۹	۱0	۵0	۱00	۵00	۱000

MYSORE, Rupee, KM-126
Regnal Year ('yr') shown

6

This coin displays the date number 1216.

Date (AM)   + 571 = Date (AD)
1216   + 571 = 1787 (AD)

Note: This coin displays the Regnal year ('yr') "6". This Regnal year has no bearing when changing the (AM) date to an (AD) date.

MYSORE, ¼ Paisa, KM-31.1

This coins displays the date number 1216.

Date (AM)   + 571 = Date (AD)
1216   + 571 = 1787 (AD)

Note: This is an example of where the Arabic (AM) date number is read from L to R.

Refer to pages: 5, 10

0	½	1	2	3	4	5	6	7	8	9	10	50	100	500	1000
0	৵	১	২	৩	8	৫	৬	৭	৮	৯	১০	৫০	১০০	৫০০	১০০০

TRIPURA, Rupee, Y-15

The Bengali date number on this coin translates to 1728.

Date (SE)   + 78 = Date (AD)
1728 (SE)   + 78 = 1806 (AD)

TRIPURA, Rupee, Y-21

The Bengali date number on this coin translates to 1731.

Date (SE)   + 78 = Date (AD)
1731 (SE)   + 78 = 1809 (AD)

DATES ON COINS OF INDIA/British

The Dating Systems used are as follows:
(AD) Christian Era — No explanation required.
(AH) Mohammedan Era — Most coins of British India, other than the (AD) dating, are according to this system. For more information on (AH) dating, refer to, "Dates on Coins of Arabic Influenced Countries".

DATES ON COINS OF INDONESIA/Java

The Dating System used is as follows:
(AS) Aki Saki — This is a Dating System that was used on but few coins about 1813-1816 (AD). Due to the many restrikes and date errors, the actual dates of the coins becomes quite confusing. From the coins listed in the SCWC which give both the (AS) and (AD) date of the coins, there is an average differential of 72.43 years. So, to establish a formula for converting (AS) dates to (AD) dates, we will assume a difference of 72 years. With this assumption, the mathematics to change an (AS) date to an (AD) date are as follows:

Calculations for (AS) Dating
Date (AS) + 72 = Date (AD)

Note: It is estimated that dating these coins could be off by as much as two years.

Refer to pages:

0	½	1	2	3	4	5	6	7	8	9	10	50	100	500	1000
o		m	૩	૨	G	૭	૮	m	૨૨	૭m	mo	૭o	moo	૭oo	mooo

JAVA, ½ Mohur, C-60

1815 (AD)

1 7 4 3
m m G ૨

The date number on this coin translates to 1743.

Date (AS)	+ 72 = Date (AD)
1743	+ 72 = 1815 (AD)

Note: It is possible to have coin dating errors by as much as two years.

1 2 3 0 (AH)

DATES ON COINS OF IRAN

The Dating System used is as follows:

(MS) Monarchic Solar Era — This is a Minor Dating System used in Iran from 2535-2537 (MS)/1976-1978 (AD). It is a Solar year system which had its numbering from the establishment of the Iranian Monarch in 559 (BC). The mathematics to change a (MS) date to an (AD) date are as follows:

Calculations for (MS) Dating
Date (MS) -559 = Date (AD)

Refer to pages: 5, 10

0	½	1	2	3	4	5	6	7	8	9	10	50	100	500	1000
•	۱/۲	۱	۲	۳	۴	۵	۶ or ۷	۷	۸	۹	۱۰	۵۰	۱۰۰	۵۰۰	۱۰۰۰

iRAN, 10 Pahlavi, Y-161

2 ۲
5 ۵
3 ۳
7 ۷

The date number on this coin translates to 2537.

Date (MS)	-559 = Date (AD)
2537	-559 = 1978 (AD)

DATES ON COINS OF ISRAEL

The Dating System used is as follows:

(JE) Jewish Era — This Dating System had its beginning on October 7, 3761 (BC) which, according to their religious beliefs, was the time of Creation.

Calculations for (JE) Dating
Date (JE) -3760 = Date (AD)

Note No. 1 — The Hebrew Calendar is now up to well over 5700 (JE) years and on most coins, the first 5000 years is left off the coin date, and is merely assumed. For example: A coin with the (JE) date of 5734 would have the date displayed on the coin as 734. The earlier coins are dated this way until 1981 where they now have the additional 5000 years included in the date.

Note No. 2 — As the Hebrew New Year occurs in the autumn of the (AD) year, it is possible to have Israeli coins with two different (JE) dates for the same (AD) year. For

ISRAEL
(JE) JEWISH ERA
HEBREW

example: If an Israeli coin was minted in that part of an (AD) year before the Hebrew New Year, it would have one (JE) year, but if a coin was minted in the same (AD) year, only after the Hebrew New Year, it could have the succeeding (JE) year.

Refer to pages: 5, 10, 14

0	½	1	2	3	4	5	6	7	8	9	10	50	100	500	1000
		א	ב	ג	ד	ה	ו	ז	ח	ט	י	נ	ק	תק	
			20	30		40	60	70	80	90	200	300	400	600	700
		ך	כ	ל	מ	ס	ע	פ	צ	ר	ש or שׂ	ש or ת	ת	תר	שת

ISRAEL, 500 Prutot, Y-14

9 — ט
Sep. Mk. — ש (300)
400 — ת

This is an example of the use of the separation mark. The separation mark is not a number.

The Hebrew date numbers on this coin translate to 709. 709 + (5000) = 5709.

The Hebrew Conversion Table, chart D, indicates 1949 (AD).

Note: Read Hebrew from R to L.

400 + 300 + 9 = 709
709 + (5000) = (5) 709 or 5709 (JE)

Date (JE)   -3760 = Date (AD)
(5) 709   -3760 = 1949 (AD)

ISRAEL, ½ Shekels, Y-29

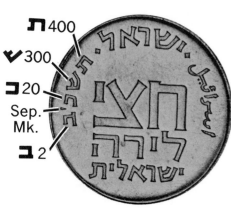

ת 400
✔ 300
ב 20
Sep. Mk.
ב 2

This is an example of the use of the separation mark. The separation mark is not a number.

The Hebrew date numbers on this coin translate to 722. 722 + (5000) = 5722

The Hebrew Conversion Table, chart D, indicates 1962 (AD).

Note: Read Hebrew from R to L.

400 + 300 + 20 + 2 = 722
722 + (5000) = (5) 722 or 5722 (JE)

Date (JL)   -3760 = Date (AD)
(5) 722   -3760 = 1962 (AD)

Refer to pages: 5, 10, 14

0	½	1	2	3	4	5	6	7	8	9	10	50	100	500	1000
		א	ב	ג	ד	ה	ו	ז	ח	ט	י	נ	ק	תק	תת

	20	30		40	60	70	80	90	200	300	400	600	700
ך	or כ	ל	מ or ם	ס	ע	פ	ף	צ	ר	or ש / שׂ	ת תר	שת	שת

ISRAEL, 100 Prutot, Y-10a.2

This is an example when using the Hebrew number Yod (10).
The Hebrew date numbers on this coin translate to 714. 714 + (5000) = 5714.
The Hebrew Conversion Table, chart D, indicates 1954 (AD).
Note: Read Hebrew from R to L.
400 + 300 + 10 + 4 = 714
714 + (5000) = (5) 714 or 5714 (JE)

Date (JE)	-3760 = Date (AD)
(5) 714	-3760 = 1954 (AD)

4   400
ד   10 (Yod)   300   ת
          ש

ISRAEL, 10 Prutot, Y-5a

This is an example when using the Hebrew number Yod (10).
The Hebrew date numbers on this coin translate to 717. 717 + (5000) = 5717.
The Hebrew Conversion Table, chart D, indicates 1957 (AD).
Note: Read Hebrew from R to L.
400 + 300 + 10 + 7 = 717
717 + (5000) = (5) 717 or 5717 (JE)

Date (JE)	-3760 = Date (AD)
(5) 717	-3760 = 1957 (AD)

7   400
ד   10 (Yod)   300   ת
          ש

DATES ON COINS OF ITALY

The Dating System used is as follows:

(YrD) Year of Dictator — A few series of Italian coins have 'yr' numbers in Roman numerals that indicate a year after Benito Mussolini took over the government. They have no relation to the Reign of King Victor Emanuel III (1900-1946 AD).

Calculations for (YrD) Dating

Beginning date	+ 'yr' = Date (AD)
1922	+ 'yr' = Date (AD)

Conversion Table
'yr' numbers/Date (AD)

The following list is taken from the Standard Catalog of World Coins and as you can see, there is much confusion. In some cases, there is more than one (AD) date that corresponds to the same 'yr' number. The reason for this is not known.

'yr'	Date (AD)	'yr'	Date (AD)	'yr'	Date (AD)
V	1927	XII	1934	XVIII	1938
VI	1927	XIII	1935	XVIII	1939
VI	1928	XIV	1936	XVIII	1940
VII	1929	XV	1937	XIX	1940
VIII	1930	XVI	1937	XIX	1941
IX	1931	XVI	1938	XX	1941
X	1931	XVII	1938	XX	1942
X	1932	XVII	1939	XXI	1943
XI	1933				

Refer to page: 96

0	½	1	2	3	4	5	6	7	8	9	10	50	100	500	1000
		I	II	III	IV	V	VI	VII	VIII	IX	X	L	C	D	M

ITALY, 20 Lira, Y-69

6 (VI)

The 'yr' number on this coin (in Roman numerals) translates to 6.

From the 'yr' Conversion Table, page 96, 'yr' 6 indicates either 1927 (AD) or 1928 (AD).

Beginning date	+ 'yr' = Date (AD)
1922	+ 6 = 1927/8 (AD)
Beginning date	= 1922 (AD)

Refer to page: 96

0	½	1	2	3	4	5	6	7	8	9	10	50	100	500	1000
		I	II	III	IV	V	VI	VII	VIII	IX	X	L	C	D	M

ITALY, Lira, Y-81

14 (XIV)

The 'yr' number on this coin (in Roman numerals) translates to 14.
From the 'yr' Conversion Table, page 96, 'yr' 14 indicates either 1935 (AD) or 1936 (AD).

Beginning date + 'yr' = Date (AD)
1922 + 14 = 1935/6 (AD)
Beginning date = 1922 (AD)

DATES ON COINS OF JAPAN

The Japanese have minted coins for centuries in various shapes, sizes and weights and, for the most part, were very much like the early Chinese coins. This early Japanese currency was a hodge-podge of precious and semi-precious metals, both cast and struck, with no standardized value. The bartering value for goods, using these coins, was based on the weight of the coin, the fineness of the metal used, the quality of the coin, and one's trading ability. This system continued through the Feudal and Shogun eras into the late 1800's, when the first decimal coinage was introduced ('yr' 3 MEIJI 1870 AD).

The Dating System used is as follows:
(YR) Year of Reign — This Dating System had its beginning in 'yr' 3 of the MEIJI REIGN (1870 AD). When a new Emperor comes into power, the first year, or part of a year, is 'yr' 1 of his reign and another 'yr' is added for each succeeding year until the end of his reign. This Dating System completed the MEIJI REIGN, progressed through the entire TAISHO REIGN, and is well along in the SHOWA REIGN (Emperor Hirohito).

Calculations for (YR) Dating
Accession date + 'yr' -1 = Date (AD)

Period Dating — The earliest Japanese cash copper square holed cash coins had no date on them and the closest accuracy is to say they were minted from 708 to 958 AD.

Then around 1580 production resumed with the last coin of this type being minted in 1869 just prior to the introduction of die struck coinage.

JAPAN
PERIOD DATING
EARLY

MAMIETA 'BEAN' GIN (Silver-Ag)

'BUN'
GENBUN PERIOD
1736-1741
(Used 1736-1818)

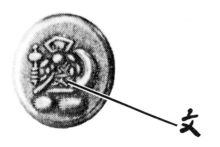

'BUN'
BUNSEI PERIOD
1818-1830
(Used 1820-1837)

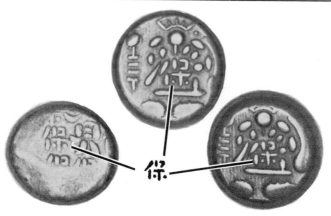

'HO'
TEMPO PERIOD
1830-1844
(Used 1837-1858)

MAMIETA 'BEAN' GIN (Silver-Ag)

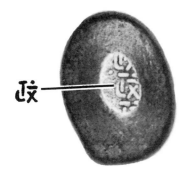

'SEI'
ANSEI PERIOD
1854-1860
(Used 1859-1865)

CHO GIN (Long) (Silver-Ag)

'BUN'
GENBUN PERIOD
1736-1741 (Used 1736-1818)

'BUN'
BUNSEI PERIOD
1818-1830 (Used 1820-1837)

'HO'
TEMPO PERIOD
1830-1844 (Used 1837-1858)

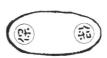

'SEI'
ANSEI PERIOD
1854-1860 (Used 1859-1865)

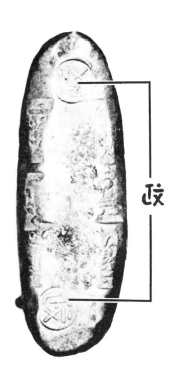

JAPAN
PERIOD DATING
EARLY

(One) (Weight) (Silver-Ag)

IS — SHU GIN

一 1
朱 Shu
銀 Ag

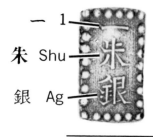
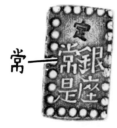

KAEI PERIOD
1848-1854
(Used 1853-1865)

常

一 1
朱 Shu
銀 Ag

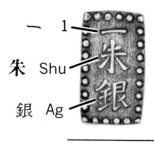
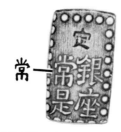

MEIJI PERIOD
1868-1912
(Used 1868-1869)

常

(One) (Weight) (Silver-Ag)

ICHI — BU GIN

一 1
分 Bu
銀 Ag

TEMPO PERIOD
1830-1844
(Used 1837-1854)

是

一 1
分 Bu
銀 Ag

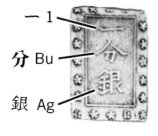

ANSEI PERIOD
1854-1860
(Used 1859-1868)

是

1 Ryo = 4 BU + 16 Shu
1 Bu = 4 Shu

ICHI — BU GIN

**MEIJI PERIOD
1868-1912**

一 1

分 Bu

銀 Ag

是

定常是銀ノ坐

**(Two) (Weight) (Silver-Ag)
NIS — SHU GIN**

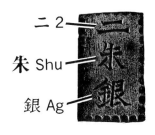

**ANSEI PERIOD
1854-1860
(Used 1859-1868)**

二 2

朱 Shu

銀 Ag

常是

**(One) (Weight) (Gold-Au)
IS — SHU KIN**

朱 Shu — 1 —

**No visible date mark
(1824-32)**

**(Two) (Weight) (Gold-Au)
NIS — SHU KIN**

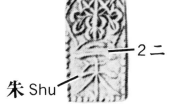

2 二

朱 Shu

**No visible date mark
(1832-58)**

1 Ryo = 4 Bu = 16 Shu
1 Bu = 4 Shu

JAPAN
PERIOD DATING
EARLY

(One) (Weight) (Gold-Au)

ICHI — BU KIN

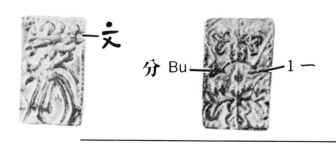

GENBUN PERIOD
1736-1741
(Used 1737-1818)

分 Bu — 1 一

BUNSEI PERIOD
1818-1830
TYPE A DATE MARK
(Used 1818-1828)

文

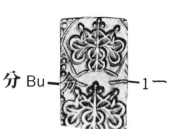

BUNSEI PERIOD
1818-1830
TYPE B DATE MARK
(Used 1819-1832)

分 Bu — 1 一

TEMPO PERIOD
1830-1844
(Used 1837-1858)

分 Bu — 1 一

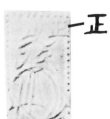
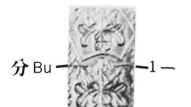

ANSEI PERIOD
1854-1860
(Used 1859)

分 Bu — 1 一

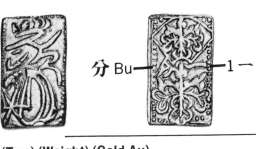

No Date
(1860-67)

分 Bu —— 1 一

(Two) (Weight) (Gold-Au)

NI — BU KIN

文 No Example

GENBUN PERIOD
1736-1741
(Used 1737-1818)

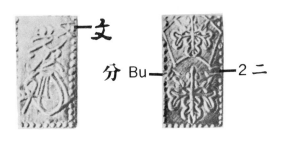

—文

分 Bu — 2 二

BUNSEI PERIOD
1818-1830
TYPE A DATE MARK
(Used 1818-1828)

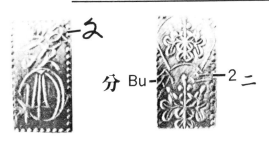

— 又

分 Bu — 2 二

BUNSEI PERIOD
1818-1830
TYPE B DATE MARK
(Used 1819-1832)

保 No Examples

TEMPO PERIOD
1830-1844
(Used 1837-1858)

1 Ryo = 4 Bu = 16 Shu
1 Bu = 4 Shu

No Example

ANSEI PERIOD
1854-1860
(Used 1859)

MANEN PERIOD
1860-1861
(Used 1860)

分   No Example

MEIJI PERIOD
1868-1912
(Used 1868-1869)

Monetary System
1 Ryo = 4 Bu = 16 Shu
1 Bu   = 4 Shu

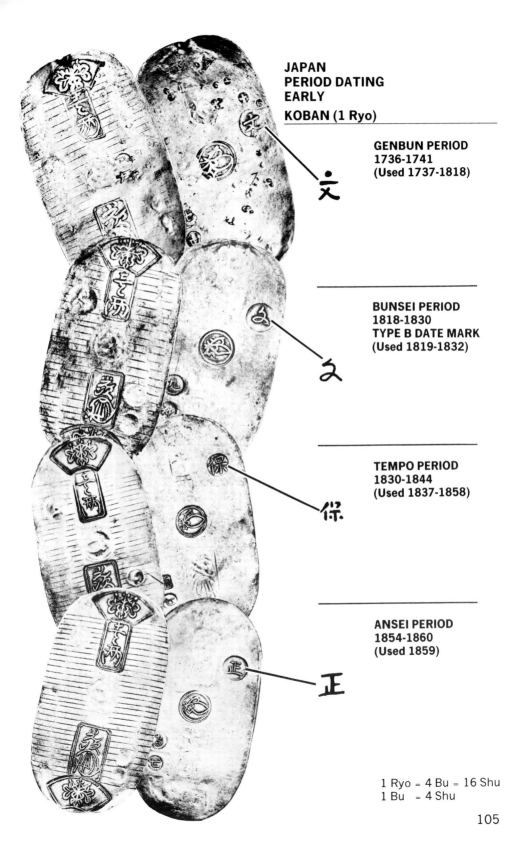

**JAPAN
PERIOD DATING
EARLY**

KOBAN (1 Ryo)

**GENBUN PERIOD
1736-1741
(Used 1737-1818)**

文

**BUNSEI PERIOD
1818-1830
TYPE B DATE MARK
(Used 1819-1832)**

文

**TEMPO PERIOD
1830-1844
(Used 1837-1858)**

保

**ANSEI PERIOD
1854-1860
(Used 1859)**

正

1 Ryo = 4 Bu = 16 Shu
1 Bu = 4 Shu

DATES ON COINS OF JAPAN

Conversion Table
'yr' number/Japanese 'yr' number/Date (AD)
MEIJI REIGN (Emperor Mutsuhito 1868-1912 AD)
Accession date = 1868 (AD)

'yr'		(AD)	'yr'		(AD)	'yr'		(AD)
3	三	1870	18	八十	1885	32	二十三	1899
4	四	1871	19	九十	1886	33	三十三	1900
5	五	1872	20	十二	1887	34	四十三	1901
6	六	1873	21	一十二	1888	35	五十三	1902
7	七	1874	22	二十二	1889	36	六十三	1903
8	八	1875	23	三十二	1890	37	七十三	1904
9	九	1876	24	四十二	1891	38	八十三	1905
10	十	1877	25	五十二	1892	39	九十三	1906
11	一十	1878	26	六十二	1893	40	十四	1907
12	二十	1879	27	七十二	1894	41	一十四	1908
13	三十	1880	28	八十二	1895	42	二十四	1909
14	四十	1881	29	九十二	1896	43	三十四	1910
15	五十	1882	30	十三	1897	44	四十四	1911
16	六十	1883	31	一十三	1898	45	五十四	1912
17	七十	1884						

Accession date + **'yr' -1 = Date (AD)**
1868 + **'yr' -1 = Date (AD)**

Refer to pages: 7, 15, 107

0	½	1	2	3	4	5	6	7	8	9	10	50	100	500	1000
零	半	一	二	三	四	五	六	七	八	九	十	十五	百	百五	千
		壹	貳	叁	肆	伍	陸	柒	捌	玖	拾	拾伍	佰	佰伍	仟

JAPAN, 50 Sen, Y-25

Mei
Ji
六
6

MEIJI REIGN (Mutsuhito 1868-1912 AD)
The 'yr' number on this coin translates to 6.
From 'yr' Conversion Table, page 107, 'yr' 6
indicates 1873 (AD).

Accession date	+ 'yr' -1	= Date (AD)
1868	+ 6 -1	= 1873 (AD)
Accession date	= 1868 (AD)	

Note: Read Japanese R to L prior to 1948 (AD).

year

JAPAN, ½ Sen, Y-16

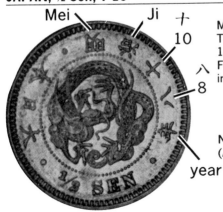

Mei
Ji
十
10
八
8

MEIJI REIGN (Mutsuhito 1868-1912 AD)
The 'yr' number on this coin translates to 18.
10 + 8 = 18
From 'yr' Conversion Table, page 107, 'yr' 16
indicates 1883 (AD).

Accession date	+ 'yr' -1	= Date (AD)
1868	+ 18 -1	= 1885 (AD)
Accession date	= 1868 (AD)	

Note: Read Japanese R to L prior to 1948 (AD).

year

DATES ON COINS OF JAPAN

Conversion Table
'yr' number/Japanese 'yr' number/Date (AD)
TAISHO REIGN (Emperor Yoshihito 1912-1926 (AD)
Accession date = 1912 (AD)

'yr'		(AD)	'yr'		(AD)	'yr'		(AD)
1	一	1912	6	六	1917	11	一十	1922
2	二	1913	7	七	1918	12	二十	1923
3	三	1914	8	八	1919	13	三十	1924
4	四	1915	9	九	1920	14	四十	1925
5	五	1916	10	十	1921	15	五十	1926

Accession date + 'yr' -1 = Date (AD)
1912   + 'yr' -1 = Date (AD)

Refer to pages: 7-15, 109

0	½	1	2	3	4	5	6	7	8	9	10	50	100	500	1000
零	半	一	二	三	四	五	六	七	八	九	十	十五	百	百五	千
		壹	貳	叁	肆	伍	陸	柒	捌	玖	拾	拾伍	佰	佰伍	仟

JAPAN, 50 Sen, Y-6

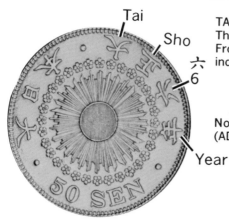

Tai
Sho
六
6
Year

TAISHO REIGN (Yoshihito 1912-1926 AD)
The 'yr' number on this coin translates to 6.
From 'yr' Conversion Table, page 109, 'yr' 6
indicates 1917 (AD).

Accession date + 'yr' -1 = Date (AD)
1912   + 6 -1 = 1917 (AD)
Accession date = 1912 (AD)
Note: Read Japanese R to L prior to 1948
(AD).

Refer to pages: 7-15, 109

0	½	1	2	3	4	5	6	7	8	9	10	50	100	500	1000
零	半	一	二	三	四	五	六	七	八	九	十	十五	百	百五	千
		壹	貳	叁	肆	伍	陸	柒	捌	玖	拾	拾伍	佰	佰伍	仟

JAPAN, Sen, Y-42

Year — 8 八 — Sho — Tai

TAISHO REIGN (Yoshihito 1912-1926 AD)
The 'yr' number on this coin translates to 10.
80 + 2 = 10.
From 'yr' Conversion Table, page 109, 'yr' 12
indicates 1923 (AD).

Accession date + 'yr' -1 = Date (AD)
1912 + 8 -1 = 1919 (AD)
Accession date = 1912 (AD)

Note: Read Japanese R to L prior to 1948
(AD).

DATES ON COINS OF JAPAN

Conversion Table
'yr' number/Japanese 'yr' number/Date (AD)
SHOWA REIGN (Emperor Hirohito 1926 -)
Accession date = 1926 (AD)

'yr'		(AD)	'yr'		(AD)	'yr'		(AD)
1	一	1926	9	九	1934	16	六十	1941
2	二	1927	10	十	1935	17	七十	1942
3	三	1928	11	一十	1936	18	八十	1943
4	四	1929	12	二十	1937	19	九十	1944
5	五	1930	13	三十	1938	20	十二	1945
6	六	1931	14	四十	1939	21	一十二	1946
7	七	1932	15	五十	1940	22	二十二	1947
8	八	1933						

'yr'		(AD)	'yr'		(AD)	'yr'		(AD)
	(Read L to R)		35	三十五	1960	48	四十八	1973
23	二十三	1948	36	三十六	1961	49	四十九	1974
24	二十四	1949	37	三十七	1962	50	五十	1975
25	二十五	1950	38	三十八	1963	51	五十一	1976
26	二十六	1951	39	三十九	1964	52	五十二	1977
27	二十七	1952	40	四十	1965	53	五十三	1978
28	二十八	1953	41	四十一	1966	54	五十四	1979
29	二十九	1954	42	四十二	1967	55	五十五	1980
30	三十	1955	43	四十三	1968	56	五十六	1981
31	三十一	1956	44	四十四	1969	57	五十七	1982
32	三十二	1957	45	四十五	1970	58	五十八	1983
33	三十三	1958	46	四十六	1971	59	五十九	1984
34	三十四	1959	47	四十七	1972	60	六十	1985

Note: The Japanese number characters (dates) are read from right to left through the year 1947 (AD). The 1948 (AD), and later, are read from left to right.

Accession date + 'yr' -1 = **Date (AD)**
1926 + 'yr' -1 = **Date (AD)**

Refer to pages: 7-15, 109

0	½	1	2	3	4	5	6	7	8	9	10	50	100	500	1000
零	半	一	二	三	四	五	六	七	八	九	十	十五	百	百五	千
		壹	貳	叁	肆	伍	陸	柒	捌	玖	拾	拾伍	佰	佰伍	仟

JAPAN, 100 Yen, Y-86

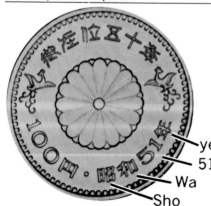
year
51
Wa
Sho

SHOWA REIGN (hirohito 1926- AD)
The 'yr' number on this coin (in western numerals) is 51.
From 'yr' Conversion Table, page 110, 'yr' 51 indicates 1976 (AD).

Accession date + 'yr' -1 = Date (AD)
1926 + 51 -1 = 1976 (AD)
Accession date = 1926 (AD)

Refer to pages: **7-15, 110**

0	½	1	2	3	4	5	6	7	8	9	10	50	100	500	1000
零	半	一	二	三	四	五	六	七	八	九	十	十五	百	百五	千
		壹	貳	叁	肆	伍	陸	柒	捌	玖	拾	拾伍	佰	佰伍	仟

JAPAN, 50 Yen, Y-76

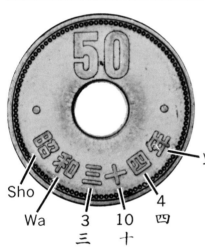

SHOWA REIGN (Hirohito 1926- AD)
The 'yr' number on this coin translates to 34.
(3 x 10) + 4 = 34.
From 'yr' Conversion Table, page 110, 'yr' 34
indicates 1959 (AD).

Accession date + 'yr' -1 = Date (AD)
1926   + 34 -1 = 1959 (AD)
Accession date = 1926 (AD)
Note: Read Japanese L to R after 1947 (AD).

year

Sho

Wa   3   10   四

3   十

4

DATES ON COINS OF KOREA

The Dating Systems used are as follows:
(KK) Kingdom of Koryo/Yi Dynasty — This Dating System had its beginning in 1392 (AD), at the time the Yi Dynasty assumed power from the Kingdom of Koryo. The Accession date is 1392 (AD).

Calculations for (KK) Dating
Date (KK)   + 'yr' -1 = Date (AD)
1392   + 'yr' -1 = Date (AD)

Note: Study the 'yr' number of Example No. 1 (KK) as to better understand large Chinese numbers.
(YR) Year of Reign — The Kuang Mu Reign was from (1897-1907 AD) and 1897 is the Accession date. The Yung Hi Reign was from (1907-1910 AD) and the Accession date is 1907 (AD).

Calculations for (YR) Dating
Accession date + 'yr' -1 = Date (AD)

KOREA
(KK) KINGDOM OF KOREA
CHINESE

Refer to pages: 15

0	½	1	2	3	4	5	6	7	8	9	10	50	100	500	1000
零	半	一	二	三	四	五	六	七	八	九	十	十五	百	百五	千
		壹	貳	叁	肆	伍	陸	柒	捌	玖	拾	拾伍	佰	佰伍	仟

KOREA, 10 Mun, Y-2

year 7
七
10
十
9
九
100
百
4
四

The 'yr' number on this coin translates to 4, 100, 9, 10 and 7. Now, to make this a useable number, do as follows:

(4 x 100) + (9 x 10) + 7 = 'yr' number
400 + 90 + 7 = 497

Accession date + 'yr' -1 = Date (AD)
1392 + 497 -1 = 1888 (AD)

The Accession date, 1392 (AD), was the year the Yi Dynasty assumed power from the Kingdom of Koryo.

Note: Read Chinese from R to L.

Kae Kuk (founding of the dynasty)

KOREA, Whan, Y-9

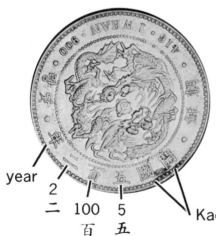

year 2
二
100
百
5
五

The 'yr' number on this coin translates to 5, 100, and 2. Now, to make this a useable number, do as follows:

(5 x 100) + 2 = 'yr' number
500 + 2 = 502

Accession date + 'yr' -1 = Date (AD)
1392 + 502 -1 = 1893 (AD)

The Accession date, 1392 (AD), was the year the Yi Dynasty assumed power from the Kingdom of Koryo.

Note: Read Chinese from R to L.

Kae Kuk (founding of the dynasty)

Refer to pages: 7-15

0	½	1	2	3	4	5	6	7	8	9	10	50	100	500	1000
零	半	一	二	三	四	五	六	七	八	九	十	十五	百	百五	千
		壹	貳	叁	肆	伍	陸	柒	捌	玖	拾	拾伍	佰	佰伍	仟

KOREA, ½ Won, Y-27

The 'yr' number on this coin translates to 2.

Accession date + 'yr' -1 = Date (AD)

1907 + 2 -1 = 1908 (AD)

This coin was minted in 'yr' 2 of the Yung Hi Reign (1907-1910) and 1907 (AD) is the Accession date.

KOREA, ½ Won, Y-18

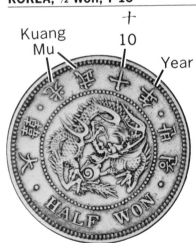

The 'yr' number on this coin translates to 10.

Accession date + 'yr' -1 = Date (AD)

1897 + 10 -1 = 1906 (AD)

This coin was minted in 'yr' 10 of the Kuang Mu Reign (1897-1907) and 1897 (AD) is the Accession date.

DATES ON COINS OF SOUTH KOREA

The Dating System used is as follows:

(KE) Korean Era — This Dating System had its beginning in 2333 (BC), with the establishment of the first Korean Dynasty. To change a (KE) date to an (AD) date, subtract 2333 from the (KE) date.

Calculations for (KE) Dating
Date (KE) -2333 = Date (AD)

Refer to pages: 5

0	½	1	2	3	4	5	6	7	8	9	10	50	100	500	1000

S. KOREA, 50 Hwan, Y-2

4294

The date (KE) on this coin (in western numerals) is 4294.

Date (KE)   -2333 = Date (AD)
4294 (KE)   -2333 = 1961 (AD)

S. KOREA, 100 Hwan, Y-3

4292

The date (KE) on this coin (in western numerals) is 4292.

Date (KE)   -2333 = Date (AD)
4292 (KE)   -2333 = 1959 (AD)

DATES ON COINS OF MONGOLIA

The Dating System used is as follows:

(YrRep) Year of the Republic — This Dating System had its beginning in 1911, the first year of the new Republic, and 1911 also is 'yr' 1 of the Republic.

Calculations for (YrRep) Dating

Beginning of

Republic	+ 'yr' 1- = Date (AD)
1911 (Yr Rep)	+ 'yr' 1- = Date (AD)

The 'yr' number found on the coin is the year during the Republic that the coin was minted.

Refer to pages: 7-15

0	½	1	2	3	4	5	6	7	8	9	10	50	100	500	1000
O	%ર	၅	၉	၃	၁	၅	၆	၈	၆	૯	၅၀	၅၀	၅၀၀	၅၀၀	၅၀၀၀

MONGOLIA, 2 Mongo, Y-2

1   5
ဂ   ၅

The 'yr' number on this coin translates to 15.

(Beginning of

Republic)	+ 'yr' -1 = Date (AD)
1911	+ 15 -1 = 1925 (AD)

MONGOLIA, 20 Mongo, Y-15

2   7
ၐ   ၈

The 'yr' number on this coin translates to 27.

(Beginning of

Republic)	+ 'yr' -1 = Date (AD)
1911	+ 27 -1 = 1937 (AD)

DATES ON COINS OF NEPAL

The Dating Systems used are as follows:

(SE) Saka Era — This Dating System had its beginning on March 3, 78 (AD) and to change a (SE) date to an (AD) date, add 78 to the (SE) date.

Calculations for (SE) Dating

Date (SE) + 78 = Date (AD)

(VS) Vikrama Samvat Era — This Dating System is the most widely used in Nepal and it had its beginning on October 18, 58 (BC). To change a (VS) date to an (AD) date, subtract 57 from the (VS) date.

Calculations for (VS) Dating

Date (VS) -57 = Date (AD)

There is a wide variation of the graphic designs of Nepalese numerals. For alternate possibilities, see the chart below.

NUMERALS

There is a wide variation of the graphic designs of Nepalese numerals. For alternate possibilities, see the chart at right. Nepal has used more variations of numerals on their coins than any other nation. The commonest are illustrated in the numeral chart in the introduction. This chart illustrates some variations encompassing the last four centuries.

1	2	3	4	5	6	7	8	9	0

Refer to pages: 5, 10

0	½	1	2	3	4	5	6	7	8	9	10	50	100	500	1000

NEPAL, ¼ Mohar, Y-13a

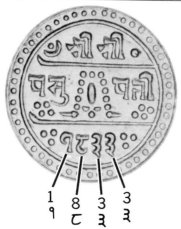

The date (SE) number on this coin translates to 1833.

Date (SE)   + 78 = Date (AD)
1833 (SE)   + 78 = 1911 (AD)

Refer to pages: 5, 10

0	½	1	2	3	4	5	6	7	8	9	10	50	100	500	1000
०	९⁄२	११ or	२	३	४	४४ or	६	७	८८	६६ or	९०	४०	९००	४००	९०००

NEPAL, Mohar, Y-15b

The date (SE) number on this coin translates to 1831.

Date (SE)	+ 78 =	Date (AD)
1831 (SE)	+ 78 =	1909 (AD)

Refer to pages: 5, 10

NEPAL, 2 Paisa, Y-8

The date (VS) number on this coin translates to 1968.

Date (VS)	-57 =	Date (AD)
1968 (VS)	-57 =	1911 (AD)

NEPAL
(VS) VIKRAMA SAMVAT
NEPALESE

Refer to pages: 5, 10

0	½	1	2	3	4	5	6	7	8	9	10	50	100	500	1000
0	⅟₂	१९	२	३	४	૪५	६	७	८ट	६६	९0	५0	९00	५00	९000

NEPAL, 2 Mohars, Y-35

1 9 8 8
१ ट ट

The date (VS) number on this coin translates to 1988.

Date (VS)	-57 = Date (AD)
1988 (VS)	-57 = 1931 (AD)

OTTOMAN EMPIRE

This huge Turkish Empire (1754-1923 AD), at one time or another, controlled all of Asia Minor, most of the near East, almost all of the north African countries and a good portion of southeastern Europe. The countries affected were:

Albania
Algeria
Egypt
Greece (Crete & Cyprus)
Iraq
Jordan
Lebanon
Libya
Romania
Saudi Arabia
Syria
Tunisia
Yugoslavia

It is wise when dating coins of these countries to carefully read the preambles in the appropriate section of your SCWC, to see what affect the Turkish coin dating system had. The Turkish system used the (YR) Year of Reign dating almost exclusively.

(YR) Year of Reign Coin Dating

(YR) Year of Reign — This is a dating system where coins are dated according to the reign of some emperor, king or ruler. The year, or part of a year, when the ruler assumed power is called the Accession date, and is 'yr' 1 of the reign. The 'yr' is increased by one for each succeeding year that ruler is in power. This 'yr' number found on the coin also denotes the particular year during the reign when the coin was minted. Almost all Turkish coins which were dated according to the (YR) system has the Accession date displayed on all coins minted during the reign of a ruler.

The mathematics to determine a (YR) date are as follows:

(YR) Dating System
Accession date + 'yr' on coin -1 = Date (AD)

Note: See section "Why Do We Subtract 1?".

Refer to pages: 5, 10, 16

0	½	1	2	3	4	5	6	7	8	9	10	50	100	500	1000
•	١/٢	١	٢	٣	٤	٥	٦	٧	٨	٩	١٠	٥٠	١٠٠	٥٠٠	١٠٠٠

TURKEY, 1½ Altin, C-27

Mahmud I (1730-1754) 1143-1168 AH.
Accession date: ١١٤٣ / 1143 AH / 1730 AD
Note: Initial letters were used in place of regnal year numerals for the coinage of Mahmud I.

1 1 4 3
١ ١ ٤ ٣

EGYPT, Zeri Mahbub, C-19

Osman III (1754-1757 AD) 1168-1171 AH.
Accession date: ١١٦٨ / 1168 AH / 1754 AD.
Note: Initial letters were used in place of regnal year numerals for the coinage of Osman III. Refer to chart in Standard Catalog of World Coins.

1 1 6 8
١ ١ ٦ ٨

Initial letter

OTTOMAN EMPIRE
YEAR OF REIGN
ARABIC

Refer to pages: 5, 10, 16

0	½	1	2	3	4	5	6	7	8	9	10	50	100	500	1000
•	١/٢	١	٢	٣	٤	٥	٦	٧	٨	٩	١٠	٥٠	١٠٠	٥٠٠	١٠٠٠

TURKEY, Piastre, C-46

Mustafa III (1757-1774 AD) 1171-1887 AH.
Accession date: ١١٧١/1171 AH/1757 AD)
The 'yr' number on this coin translates to 6.
The Accession date on this coin translates to 1171, which is a Lunar (AH) year.

Accession date + 'yr' -1 = AH Mint year

1171 AH + 6 -1 = 1176 (AH). See chart E.

Note: The last 2 digits of the actual year (AH) appear on the later coinage of Mustafa III.

TURKEY, 10 Para, C-63

Abdul Hamid I (1774-1789 AD) 1187-1203 AH.
Accession date: ١١٨٧ /1187 AH/1774 AD
The 'yr' number on this coin translates to 6.
The Accession date on this coin translates to 1187, which is a Lunar (AH) year.

Accession date + 'yr' -1 = AH Mint year

1187 + 6 -1 = 1192 (AH). See Hejira Date Chart E.

Refer to pages: 5, 10, 16

0	½	1	2	3	4	5	6	7	8	9	10	50	100	500	1000
•	١/٢	١	٢	٣	٤	٥	٦	٧	٨	٩	١•	٥•	١••	٥••	١•••

TURKEY, 10 Para, C-88

Selim III (1789-1807 AD) 1203-1222 AH.
Accession date: ١٢•٣ /1203 AH /1789 AD
The 'yr' number on this coin translates to 18.
The accession date on this coin translates to 1203, which is a Lunar (AH) year.

Accession date + 'yr' -1 = AH Mint year
1203 + 18 -1 = 1220 (AH). See Hejira Chart E.

TURKEY, 10 Para, C-113

Mustafa IV (1807-1808 AD) 1222-1223 AH.
Accession date: ١٢٢٢ /1222 AH /1807 AD
The 'yr' number on this coin translates to 1.
The Accession date on this coin translates to 1222, which is a Lunar (AH) year.

Accession date + 'yr' -1 = AH Mint year
1222 + 1 -1 = 1222 (AH). See Hejira Chart E.

OTTOMAN EMPIRE
YEAR OF REIGN
ARABIC

Refer to pages: 5, 10, 16

0	½	1	2	3	4	5	6	7	8	9	10	50	100	500	1000
٠	١/٢	١	٢	٣	٤	٥	٦	٧	٨	٩	١٠	٥٠	١٠٠	٥٠٠	١٠٠٠

TURKEY, 3 Piastres, C-207

Mahmud II (1808-1839 AD) 1223-1255 AH.
Accession date: ١٢٢٣ /1223 AH/1808 AD
The 'yr' number on this coin translates to 31.
The Accession date on this coin translates to
1223, which is a Lunar (AH) Year.

Accession date + 'yr' -1 = AH Mint year
1223   + 31 -1 = 1253 (AH). See Hejira Chart E.

TURKEY, 6 Piastres, C-271

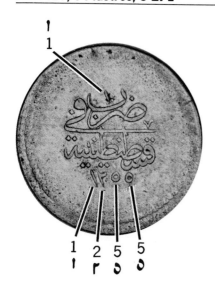

Abdul Mejid (1839-1861 AD) 1255-1277 AH.
Accession date: ١٢٥٥ /1255 AH/1839 AD
The 'yr' number on this coin translates to 1.
The Accession date on this coin translates to
1255, which is a Lunar (AH) year.

Accession date + 'yr' -1 = AH Mint year
1255   + 1 -1 = 1255 (AH). See Hejira Chart E.

Refer to pages: 5, 10, 16

0	½	1	2	3	4	5	6	7	8	9	10	50	100	500	1000
•	١/٢	١	٢	٣	٤	٥	٦	٧	٨	٩	١٠	٥٠	١٠٠	٥٠٠	١٠٠٠

TURKEY, 100 Piastres, Y-17

Abdul Aziz (1861-1876 AD) 1276-1293 AH.
Accession date: ١٢٧٧ /1277 AH/1861 AD
The 'yr' number on this coin translates to 7.
The Accession date on this coin translates to
1277, which is a Lunar (AH) year.

Accession date + 'yr' -1 = AH Mint year
1277   + 7 -1 = 1283 (AH). See Hejira Chart E.

```
1  2  7  7
١  ٢  ٧  ٧
```

```
7
٧
```

TURKEY, 100 Piastres, Y-C22

Murad V (1876 AD) 1293 AH.
Accession date: ١٢٩٣ /1293 AH/1876 AD
The 'yr' number on this coin translates to 1.
The Accession date on this coin translates to
1293, which is a Lunar (AH) year.

Accession date + 'yr' -1 = AH Mint year
1293   + 1 -1 = 1293 (AH). See Hejira Chart E.

```
1  2  9  3
١  ٢  ٩  ٣
```

```
1
١
```

123

OTTOMAN EMPIRE
YEAR OF REIGN
ARABIC

Refer to pages: 5, 10, 16

0	½	1	2	3	4	5	6	7	8	9	10	50	100	500	1000
•	١/٢	١	٢	٣	٤	٥	٦	٧	٨	٩	١٠	٥٠	١٠٠	٥٠٠	١٠٠٠

TURKEY, 5 Piastres, Y-34

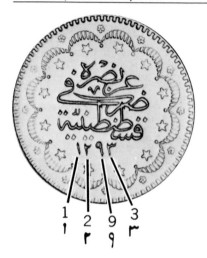

1 2 9 3
١ ٢ ٩ ٣

Abdul Hamid II (1876-1909 AD) 1293-1327 AH.
Accession date:١٢٩٣/1293 AH/1876 AD
The 'yr' number on this coin translates to 11.
The Accession date on this coin translates to 1293, which is a Lunar (AH) year.

Accession date + 'yr' -1 = AH Mint year
1293   + '11 -1 = 1303 (AH). See Hejira Chart E.

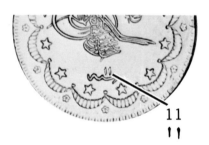

11
١١

TURKEY, 2 Piastres, Y-48

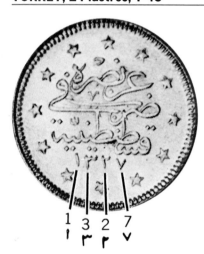

1 3 2 7
١ ٣ ٢ ٧

Muhammad V (1909-1918 AD) 1327-1336 AH.
Accession date:١٣٢٧/1327 AH/1909 AD
The 'yr' number on this coin translates to 1.
The Accession date on this coin translates to 1327, which is a Lunar (AH) year.

Accession date + 'yr' -1 = AH Mint year.
1327   + 1 -1   = 1327 (AH). See Hejira Chart E.

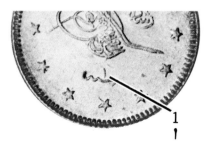

1
١

Refer to pages: 5, 10, 16

0	½	1	2	3	4	5	6	7	8	9	10	50	100	500	1000
•	١/٢	١	٢	٣	٤	٥	٦	٧	٨	٩	١٠	٥٠	١٠٠	٥٠٠	١٠٠٠

TURKEY, 20 Piastres, Y-62

Muhammad VI (1918-1923 AD) 1336-1341 AH.
Accession date: ١٣٣٦ /1336 AH/1918 AD
The 'yr' number on this coin translates to 1.
The Accession date on this coin translates to 1336, which is a Lunar (AH) year.

Accession date   + 'yr' -1 = AH Mint year

1336   + 1 -1 = 1336 AH. See Hejira Chart E.

DATES ON COINS OF THAILAND/SIAM

The Dating Systems used are as follows:

(AH) Mohammedan Era — The numbers used for (AH) dating are in Arabic. For examples and explanations of (AH) dating, refer to the sections on, "Dates on Coins of Arabic Influenced Countries".

(BE) Buddhist Era — This Dating System had its beginning in 543 (BC) and to change a (BE) date to an (AD) date, subtract 543 from the (BE) date. The date numbers will be in Thai — Lao numerals.

Calculations for (BE) Dating
Date (BE) -543 = Date (AD)

(CS) Chula-Sakarat Era — This Dating System had its beginning in 638 (AD) and to change a (CS) date to an (AD) date, add 638 to the (CS) date. The date numbers will be in Thai — Lao numerals.

Calculations for (CS) Dating
Date (CS) + 638 = Date (AD)

(RS) Bangkok Era (Ratanakosind-sok) — This Dating System had its beginning in 1781 (AD) and to change a (RS) date to an (AD) date, add 1781 to the (RS) date. The date numbers will be in Thai — Lao numerals.

Calculations for (RS) Dating
Date (RS) + 1781 = Date (AD)

THAILAND
(BE) BUDDHIST ERA
THAI-LAO

Refer to pages: 5, 10

0	½	1	2	3	4	5	6	7	8	9	10	50	100	500	1000
𝟶	%ᴗ	𝜊	๒	๓	๔	๕	๖	๗	๘	๙	๑๐	๔๐	๑๐๐	๔๐๐	๑๐๐๐

SIAM, ½ Baht, Y-44

The date (BE) number on this coin translates to 2463.

Date (BE)	-543	= Date (AD)
2463 (BE)	-543	= 1920 (AD)

THAILAND, Baht, Y-84

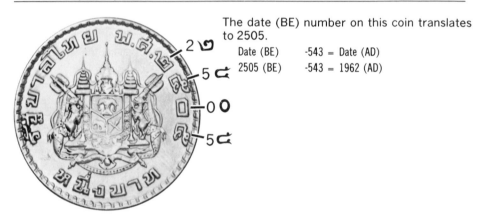

The date (BE) number on this coin translates to 2505.

Date (BE)	-543	= Date (AD)
2505 (BE)	-543	= 1962 (AD)

Refer to pages: 5, 10

0	½	1	2	3	4	5	6	7	8	9	10	50	100	500	1000
0	⁰⁄₆	๑	๒	๓	๔	๕	๖	๗	๘	๙	๑๐	๕๐	๑๐๐	๕๐๐	๑๐๐๐

SIAM, 2 Att, Y-19

The date (CS) number on this coin translates to 1244.

    Date (CS)   + 638 = Date (AD)
    1244 (CS)   + 638 = 1882 (AD)

1 2 4 4
๑ ๒ ๔ ๔

SIAM, Att, Y-18

The date (CS) number on this coin translates to 1238.

    Date (CS)   + 638 = Date (AD)
    1238 (CS)   + 638 = 1876 (AD)

1 2 3 8
๑ ๒ ๓ ๘

THAILAND
(RS) BANGKOK ERA
THAI-LAO

Refer to pages: 5, 10

0	½	1	2	3	4	5	6	7	8	9	10	50	100	500	1000
๐	๚	๑	๒	๓	๔	๕	๖	๗	๘	๙	๑๐	๕๐	๑๐๐	๕๐๐	๑๐๐๐

SIAM, 20 Satang, Y-27

The date (RS) number on this coin translates to 116.

Date (RS)   + 1781 = Date (AD)

116 (RS)   + 1781 = 1897 (AD)

SIAM, ¼ Fuang, Y-23

The date (RS) number on this coin translates to 122.

Date (RS)   + 1781 = Date (AD)

122 (RS)   + 1781 = 1903 (AD)

DATES ON COINS OF USSR/Russian Caucasia/Georgia

The Dating System used is as follows:
(dt) Direct Translation — The dates on Georgian coins are in Georgian Numerals and they translate directly to the correct (AD) date.

Calculations for (dt) Dating
Date (dt) = Date (AD)

Refer to page: 15

0	½	1	2	3	4	5	6	7	8	9	10	50	100	500	1000
		ა	ბ	გ	დ	ე	ვ	ზ	ჱ	თ	ი	ნ	რ	ფ	ჩ
		11 ია	20 კ	30 ლ	40 მ	50 ნ	60 ჲ	70 ო	80 პ	90 ჟ	100 რ	200 ს, 300 ტ	400 უ	600 ქ, 700 ღ	800 ყ

GEORGIA, 10 Dinars, C-82

The date numbers on this coin translate to 1000, 800 and 5. To make this a useable number, do as follows:

1000 + 800 + 5 = 1805 (dt)

Date (dt)	= Date (AD)
1805	= 1805 (AD)

GEORGIA, 200 Dinars, C-86

The date numbers on this coin translate to 1000, 800, 10 and 9. To make this a useable number, do as follows:

1000 + 800 + 10 + 9 = 1819 (dt)

Date (dt)	= Date (AD)
1819	= 1819 (AD)

DATES ON COINS OF USSR/Krim

The Dating System used is as follows:
(AH) Mohammedan Era — The Crimean Russia had coins dated according to the (AH) system. They will not be treated in this section, but will be included in the section, "Dates on Coins of the Arabic Influenced Countries".

DATES ON COINS OF USSR/Russian Turkestan

The Dating System used is as follows:
(AH) Mohammedan Era — The coins of Russian Turkestan were dated according to this system. They will not be treated in this section, but will be included in the section, "Dates on Coins of the Arabic Influenced Countries".

DATES ON COINS OF VIETNAM/ANNAM

The Dating Systems used are as follows:
(YR) Year of Reign — A few coins minted during the Reign of Emperor Minh Mang (1820-1841 AD) were minted with dates conforming to the (YR) Year of Reign System. As Ming Mang came into power in 1820 (AD), that is 'yr' 1 of his reign and also his Accession date.
(CD) Cyclical Dating — A few coins during the reign of Emperor Thieu Tri and during the Reign of Emperor Tu Doc were minted with dates according to the Chinese (CD) Cyclical Dating System. Refer to the Chinese Cyclical Dating System for further information.
(nd) No Date — Most coins of Vietnam/Annam had no dates.

Minh Mang
Thong Bao
1820-1841

Thieu Tri Thong Bao
1841-1847

Tu Duc Thong Bao
1848-1883

Refer to pages: 7-15

0	½	1	2	3	4	5	6	7	8	9	10	50	100	500	1000
零	半	一	二	三	四	五	六	七	八	九	十	十五	百	百五	千
		壹	貳	叁	肆	伍	陸	柒	捌	玖	拾	拾伍	佰	佰伍	仟

VIETNAM/Annam, Piastre, Sch-181

3　10
三　十

Note: Read Chinese R to L.
The 'yr' number on this coin translates to (10 + 3) = 15.

Accession date　+ 'yr' -1 = Date (AD)
1820　　　　+ 13 -1 = 1832 (AD)

This coin was minted during the Reign of Minh Mang (1820-1841 AD) and his Accession date is 1820 (AD).

VIETNAM/Annam, Piastre, Sch-182

4　10
四　十

Note: Read Chinese R to L.
The 'yr' number on this coin translates to (10 + 4) = 14.

Accession date　+ 'yr' -1 = Date (AD)
1820　　　　+ 14 -1 = 1833 (AD)

This coin was minted during the Reign of Minh Mang (1820-1841 AD) and his Accession date is 1820 (AD).

131

VIETNAM/Annam
(CD) CYCLICAL DATING
CHINESE

Refer to pages: 5, 20, 21

0	½	1	2	3	4	5	6	7	8	9	10	50	100	500	1000
零	半	一	二	三	四	五	六	七	八	九	十	十五	百	百五	千
		壹	貳	叁	肆	伍	陸	柒	捌	玖	拾	拾伍	佰	佰伍	仟

VIETNAM/Annam, 10 Lang, Sch-

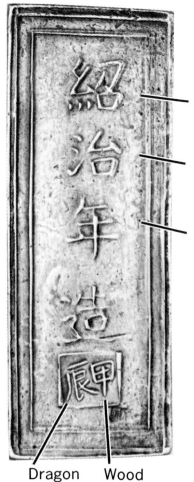

This coin indicates the 'Cyclical Year' of the 'Wood-Dragon'.
From (CD) chart H and (CD) Table, chart G.
'Wood-Dragon' = 1844 (AD)

Thieu

Tri

year

Dragon
辰

Wood
甲

CHRONOGRAMS

One of the most interesting forms of dating to appear on coins involves the use of chronograms. In particular some German thalers of the 1700's used this system. Chronogram dating presents the date hidden in a coin's Latin legends. Deciphering such dates requires removal and rearrangement of the large letters from the legends into a Roman numerical sequence.

GERMAN STATES
CHRONOGRAMS
ROMAN

0	½	1	2	3	4	5	6	7	8	9	10	50	100	500	1000
		I	II	III	IV	V	VI	VII	VIII	IX	X	L	C	D	M

TRIER, Thaler, C-89

The Roman numerals found on this coin are CLIVIXVIIIVVMIICIVDI. The logical sequence to rearrange this in is MDCCLXVVVVVIIIIIIIII. This Roman numeral date translates to 1794.

CLIVIXVIIIVVMIICIVDI

NOTES

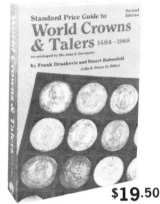
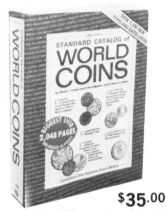

NOTES